W9-BTQ-041

The Bread Machine Cookbook IV

Donna Rathmell German

Bristol Publishing Enterprises, Inc.
San Leandro, California

A Nitty Gritty® Cookbook

Printed in the United States of America.

ISBN 1-55867-049-1

Cover design: Frank Paredes
Cover photography: John Benson

CONTENTS

Many thanks to all of the testers and tasters who made and ate hundreds of loaves of bread. A special thanks to Melody McKinley, Debbie Nicholson, Amy Peacock, Mary Vollendorf and Rhonda Lechner. This book could not have been written without the tremendous help and assistance from Megan Pyle and Shannon Mulloy to whom I express my deep gratitude.

Technical assistance was given by and is gratefully acknowledged to Sharon Davis of the Kansas Wheat Commission, and to Tom Dickson of K-Tec, Inc.

Last but not least, my family deserves many thanks for their patience with multiple bread machines running around the clock and expecially to my husband for all of his support and encouragement.

BAKING WITH WHOLE GRAINS

Baking with whole grains is substantially different than baking with refined all purpose or bread flour. Breads made with whole grains have a delicious nutty taste and a denser heavier texture. Once you have tasted loaves made with whole grains, especially those which are made with freshly milled flours, you may never again return to refined flours. I started experimenting with whole grain bread baking as the result of many questions and requests from people wanting whole grain recipes for their bread machines. Once I started milling my own flours and delving into recipe after recipe, I became hooked. I think you will be too!

Whole grain flours are flours which are not refined. Using wheat as an example, whole wheat flour is a whole grain flour while white all purpose or bread flours are refined. Whole wheat flour bought in the grocery store has been milled and refined and then had the germ and bran replaced. Wheat flour which is freshly milled and used usually does not have the germ or bran separated — they are milled into the flour from the start. These flours retain the oils from the bran and germ and may become rancid very quickly.

WHEAT: CHARACTERISTICS AND VARIETIES

A wheat berry, also called a wheat kernel or the grain of wheat, is actually a seed. These berries are what are commonly ground into flour, sprouted, cracked, flaked or may even be cooked and eaten as they are, much like rice. Wheat is a cereal grain and is a very concentrated source of protein and carbohydrates. Like rice, the protein from wheat is incomplete. It is complimented, or the protein gaps are filled in, when combined with milk or beans. The protein in wheat is also called gluten.

Each berry is made up of three parts:

- The **germ** (2½% of the berry) is the embryo of the grain itself and is a great source of vitamin E, vitamin B and some protein. This is the section of the grain which sprouts.

- The **bran** (14½% of the berry) is the outer layer of the grain which provides us with fiber, and the majority of the B vitamins as well as approximately 19% of the protein.

- The **endosperm** (83% of the berry) is the white, starchy part of the grain. After removing the germ and bran, the endosperm is what is left and used for "white" flour, whether all purpose, cake or bread. The endosperm contains approximately 70-75% of the protein.

Most of the fiber, oil and B vitamins and approximately 25% of the protein of wheat are contained in the bran and the germ. While very high sources of nutrition, both the bran and the germ reduce the elasticity of the gluten in bread baking which results in lower rising, denser, more flavorful loaves of bread. The coarser the flour from the bran and germ, the denser, more low-rising the loaf will be. The natural oils in the bran and germ become rancid very quickly. Freshly milled home flours may become rancid due to these oils. Flour begins to loose vitamin strength within 72 hours of milling.

When you look in a health food store or a mail order catalog for wheat berries, you may see several different types. Wheat itself is divided into 5 classes:

- hard red winter wheat - Used for bread baking, grown primarily in the Midwest (Kansas) with some grown in the Northwest. Protein ranges from 10-15%.
- hard red spring wheat - Used for bread baking, grown primarily in the Northwest. Protein ranges from 12-18%.
- soft red winter wheat - Used for cakes and pastries, grown primarily in the East to eastern Midwest. Protein ranges from 8-11%.
- white wheat - Used for cakes and pastries, grown primarily in the Northwest and Northeast.
- durum wheat - Used for pasta - grown primarily in the North to Midwest.

Grain used for bread baking should be **hard**. If a protein content is known, it should be 14% or higher. Flour which is milled from hard wheat is known as bread flour because of the higher protein (gluten) content. Soft wheat has a lower protein content and is generally used for cakes or pastries. Flour milled from a combination of hard and soft wheat is known as all purpose flour and generally has a protein content of 9-11%.

The protein of the wheat, and therefore the flour, is also known as gluten. Gluten becomes elastic when mixed with water or liquid. This elastic gluten forms a woven, elastic network which traps the carbon dioxide and alcohol produced by the yeast and causes the dough to rise. While other grains, such as rye, contain a small amount of gluten, it does not stretch like the wheat does which means that rye breads cannot rise as high or have as light a texture.

Winter wheat is planted in the fall, grows partially, and then lies dormant for the winter and resumes growing in the spring. Spring wheat is planted in the spring. Using red versus white or spring versus winter is a matter of preference.

The grain itself, and the resulting flour, is affected by many factors such as the variety, growing conditions (heat, cold, drought, wind, hail, frost, etc.) and geographic location. Rain (or the lack of) can severely impact the growing grain which then affects the moisture of the berry itself. Insects can have a detrimental impact upon wheat, destroying entire crops. The protein/gluten itself varies from one crop year to another.

MILLING

Milling is the process which breaks apart the wheat berry, separates the bran and germ from the endosperm and then grinds the endosperm into flour. The earliest form of milling was performed by rubbing the grain between two stones. Wind or water was harnessed and provided the means to turn the stones and mill the flour. The flour was sifted through fabric meshes which separated the bran and germ from the flour. Roller mills were introduced in the mid-1800s.

Most commercial mills today use grooved rollers which crush the grain. Coarse particles are separated by being sifted through a series of screens in a box-like structure which vibrates. Both the bran and germ are removed during this process. The process is repeated several times until the flour obtains its desired consistency.

Stone milling is still practiced by some smaller, regional flour milling companies.

This is considered by some people to be more natural and healthier. Research shows that some of the stone particles are usually combined with the flour.

It used to be that white, refined flour was, like sugar, considered pure and commanded a higher price which was only afforded by the wealthy. Due to the missing bran and germ, white flour has a longer shelf life than freshly milled flours.

Flour with the bran and germ removed may be left alone to whiten naturally, which is known as unbleached flour. Bleached flour has been treated with some bleaching agents which mature the flour and hasten getting it to the store shelves. Flours are clearly labeled bleached or unbleached. For bread baking, many people seem to prefer the unbleached. Whole wheat flour is milled in the same way, but the oil is removed from the bran and germ and they are returned to the finely ground flour.

Due to poor health and diseases during the 1930s, studies were done which examined the nutritional intake of American citizens. As a result of these studies, public health officials and departments of the U.S. government urged the addition of certain vitamins and minerals to some food groups in order to provide additional nutrition to the diets of Americans. The enrichment of flour began as a result of dietary needs and not as a function of vitamins lost during the milling process. In fact, all purpose enriched flour has some vitamin B amounts higher than whole wheat flour or wheat berries. Enrichment is the term for the addition of thiamin, niacin, riboflavin and iron. Calcium was added to the list in the 1970s.

Home milling. There are several brands of small hand or electric home mills on the market which enable us to mill our own flour when and as needed. When milling your own flour, it should be very finely milled for the lightest texture. Coarsely ground flour absorbs the water more slowly.

Types of mills available. Hand mills are usually small, with a capacity of 1 cup of grain or less at a time. They require grinding using a crank and may or may not come with a screen to separate out the bran and germ if desired. Hand mills are less expensive and I have even seen a few which roll some grains into flakes (rolled oats) which may be used in bread baking or for cereal.

Electric mills usually use stainless steel milling blades. One of the benefits of steel over stone is that moist grains or beans may be milled without gumming up the milling chamber. Soybean, for example, may be milled by steel but not by stone. Well over 10 cups of grain may be milled at a time.

SUCCESSFUL WHOLE GRAIN BREAD BAKING IN BREAD MACHINES

Flour used in the bread machine should be whole wheat bread flour or flour milled from hard winter or spring wheat. The protein (gluten) content should be 14% or higher. Finding whole wheat bread flour is difficult in most parts of the country although it may usually be ordered by mail (see Sources, page 168). Regular all purpose whole wheat flour may be used but vital gluten (optional ingredient in each recipe) should be added to it.

Gluten is what absorbs the water and since gluten levels vary according to the wheat/flour used, it follows that the flour absorbs water according to the amount of gluten in it. Flours with a higher amount of gluten require more water than that which has a lower gluten or protein count. Flours also absorb water differently according to how coarsely or finely they were milled.

During testing for this book, I noticed tremendous differences in the amount of liquids required depending on whether I used purchased whole wheat flour or freshly milled flour, or the type of grains that were used for milling my own flour. When kneading bread dough by machine, it is necessary to develop a sense of what *looks* right. If you have problems with the texture of your loaves, allow the machine to knead the dough for approximately 3 to 5 minutes and then look at the dough. If your machine has no window, it is okay to open the machine briefly to look at what is happening inside — just don't sit with it open for long periods of time. With few exceptions, the dough should form a nice, smooth ball. Sometimes the ball will be round and at other times it may be more cylindrical in shape. By watching the dough on a regular basis, you will soon develop a sense of what looks right.

If a dough is too dry, it will not mix properly. It may form two or more balls of dough or simply will not stick together. In some cases, the machine may even sound as though it is struggling to knead. If any of these events occur, simply add whatever liquid you are using, one tablespoon at a time, until the required consistency is obtained.

Conversely, dough which is too wet will not be able to form a ball and flour should be added one tablespoon at a time until a ball is formed.

Keep in mind, however, that machines are capable of kneading dough which is much moister than could be kneaded by hand. There is a fine line between what will be a great, light and airy loaf and one which will sink because of too much liquid. Experience will guide.

Recipes which use fruits or vegetables as a source of liquid should be checked about 3 to 5 minutes into the initial kneading. One fruit or vegetable may have a different moisture content than another and therefore, the dough may need additional water or flour.

If stored properly, wheat berries will last for years. Wheat berries should be stored in metal or glass containers, tightly covered in a cool, dry place. A garbage can with a tight fitting lid may be used but should not sit directly on a cement flour — try putting it on slabs of wood.

Bay leaves may be placed in the container with grain or flour to prevent insect infestation. Dry ice placed in the bottom of the container of wheat berries also fights insects by depleting the oxygen supply as the ice evaporates. Use approximately 2 oz. of dry ice per 25 lbs. of grain. The grain may also be frozen to kill any insects.

Flour may be frozen in small amounts. This is particularly important for flour which has been home-milled as the oils from both the bran and germ are still contained. After milling, I measure flour into the amounts which I use most frequently and put it in ziplock freezer bags marked with the amount and date of milling. The flour may be thawed at room temperature for 2 to 3 hours and used as needed.

When using a timer cycle for several hours during times of high heat and humidity, the liquid amount should be cut by a tablespoon or two. Salt may be increased a little to keep the dough from rising too quickly and then collapsing.

If breads are not cooking through properly and are still doughy in the middle, cover the top of the machine with aluminum foil but don't cover any air vents. This problem seems to occur most often with the DAK and Welbilt ABM 100 machines — probably because of the large glass dome. It also seems to occur with recipes which are high in fat, sugar or fruits and using the sweet cycle seems to help. In a worst-case scenario, cut the fat, fruit or sugar and adjust the liquid if necessary.

If loaves are not rising properly all of a sudden, think about what may have changed recently. Has the weather changed suddenly and you have opened windows or turned on air conditioning? Machines sitting in drafts may sometimes have difficulty. Some people have also reported that the loaves were not rising properly and they moved the machine away from the refrigerator and it worked better.

Ingredients such as rice, cheese or potatoes should be lightly packed into the measuring cup.

DOUGH ENHANCERS

Bread baking with whole grains is trickier than with refined flour as the bran and germ both restrict the gluten in its ability to form the elastic network and to expand. It is for this reason that whole grain loaves are generally lower and denser than those which use white, refined flour.

Dough enhancers are ingredients which are added to or used in whole grain bread dough with one of its main purposes to assist in achieving a higher rising, lighter loaf. Research led me to several enhancers with which I have tested with varying results. Vital gluten was used in the testing of each recipe. I mention the others as you, too, may have heard of these enhancers and may wish to add them to your doughs.

Vital gluten is the dried gluten protein which has been obtained from the flour by rinsing off the starch. This has been the most significant conditioner I have found and is included in all recipes in this book in a range as an optional ingredient. If using a machine which has a cycle geared specifically for whole grain bread baking (longer rising times) and if you use a whole wheat bread flour or flour milled from a hard (high protein/gluten) wheat, it may not be necessary to add the vital gluten. I prefer to add it in all cases but under the above conditions, I use the smallest amount.

Buttermilk is produced by adding bacterial cultures (like yogurt) called lactobacilli to either lowfat or skim milk. The milk is allowed to sit at room temperature for approximately 24 hours, similar to a sourdough culture. It is then refrigerated which slows down the bacterial action. Buttermilk is a lowfat, creamy ingredient which results in a light, high rising and tender bread. Buttermilk requires baking soda to be used to offset the slight acidity. Vinegar and lemon juice are sometimes used as dough enhancers (see page 20).

Egg protein, specifically from the yolk (contains lecithin, see page 11), has a leaving effect and adds to the structure of the bread. Add egg to liquid when measuring.

Ascorbic acid (Vitamin C) is added to some commercially milled flours to help mature the flour and to improve its breadmaking qualities. Add approximately 250 mg for each 2 cups of flour. I have found granulated vitamin C at the health food store. The strength of vitamin C I use is 2000 mg/tsp (information found on side of container). I want 250 mg so I use the following equation to determine how much to use per 2 cups of flour: $250/2000 = .125$ or ⅛ tsp. Testing was done using ⅛ tsp. of vitamin C granules in the small recipe, ⅛+ in the medium and ¼ tsp. in the large. Vitamin C tablets may be crushed, or ground with a mortar and pestle.

Lecithin is a food supplement which is obtained from the oil in egg yolks or soy beans. It improves moisture and assists in the expansion and elasticity of the bread dough. Add between 1 to 1½ tsp. of lecithin granules per cup of flour. Works well.

Malt, also called diastatic malt, is a derivative of wheat or barley. It may occasionally be found in health food stores but may also be made at home quite easily with a home mill. The barley must be whole (not pearled) and is difficult to find, so wheat may be generally what is used. Sprout (see page 42) the wheat or the barley which develops the natural sugars. The sprouts should be the length of the seed. The sprouts may then be spread on an ungreased baking pan and dried in a low (125-200°) oven for a day or so until they are completely dry. The dried, sprouted berries are then milled to a fine flour consistency in a home mill and may be kept in a tightly sealed container in the refrigerator for several months. Use approximately 1 tbs. for each cup of flour. Technically, diastatic malt may be used as a substitute for sweeteners in bread baking; however, I preferred the results in bread machines using it as a dough enhancer.

Tofu is one of the main ingredients in several "dough enhancer" products available for purchase. Tofu drink mixes are also used as enhancers in bread baking. In the products with which I have experimented, lecithin is an ingredient. Dried tofu powder alone seemed to have little impact upon the rising of the loaf. Tofu is bean curd made from soy beans. The enhancer or drink mix products seem to work well.

BIBLIOGRAPHY

Countryside Magazine (Editors). COUNTRY KITCHEN: A PROJECT & IDEA BOOK. PA: TAB Books, 1985

Gerras, Charles; Editor. RODALE'S BASIC NATURAL FOODS COOKBOOK. NY: Simon & Schuster, 1984

Goldbeck, Nikki and David. AMERICAN WHOLEGOOD CUISINE. NY: New American Library (NAL), 1983

Griswold, Ruth M. THE EXPERIMENTAL STUDY OF FOODS. (Boston) MA: Houghton Mifflin Company, 1962 La Leche League. WHOLE FOODS FOR THE WHOLE FAMILY. NY: New American Library (NAL), 1981

McGee, Harold. ON FOOD AND COOKING - THE SCIENCE AND LORE OF THE KITCHEN. NY: Charles Scribner's Sons, 1984

Robertson, Laurel, THE LAUREL'S KITCHEN BREAD BOOK. NY: Random House, 1984

Wheat Flour Institute. FROM WHEAT TO FLOUR. DC: 1981

HOW TO USE THIS BOOK

For testing purposes, the following machines were used on the listed sizes. The cycle listed is that which was used for testing whole grain baking and that which I recommend.

MACHINE	SIZES TESTED			RECOMMENDED CYCLE
DAK (regular and Turbo)	small	medium	large	sweet
Hitachi 101 and 201***	small	medium***		bread
Hitachi 301	small	medium	large	bread
National/Panasonic #5 series	small			basic/whole grain
National/Panasonic #6 series	medium	large		basic/whole grain
Magic Mill (round dome)	small	medium	large	sweet
Regal - Deluxe	small	medium		bread
Regal - K6772	small			bread
Sanyo	small			bread
Seiko/Mr. Loaf/Chefmate/Maxim	small			standard
Welbilt ABM 100 (round dome)	small	medium	large	sweet
Welbilt ABM 300, 350, 600	small			regular
Zojirushi (with jam)	small	medium	large	white
Zojiurshi (without jam)	small	medium***		white

***IMPORTANT! Since whole grain breads do not rise as high as those which are made using refined flour, recipes in this particular book may exceed the normal recommended capacities of bread or refined flour for your machine. Some recipes using fruits, cheeses, rice, peanut butter, potatoes or a much higher amount of flour may require the side of the pan to be scraped to assist the ingredients being picked up by the kneading paddle. If making a medium or large recipe with any of these ingredients, I strongly recommend checking the dough approximately 5 minutes into the kneading cycle to ensure that the ingredients are being well blended. If wanting to use a timer, I recommend using the next size smaller. We found that the few times it was necessary to scrape the ingredients off the side of the pan to assist the blending, it was usually in the Hitachi or the new Zojirushi (without the jam) machines. If in doubt, use the next smaller size than usual. We did not have this problem with the small size recipes.

National/Panasonic machines: Due to the shape of the pan, I find that using a medium or large size recipe in the 1.5 lb. machine works quite well; however I do not recommend using the small size recipe.

Seiko, Mister Loaf, Chefmate, Maxim machines seemed to provide a better loaf of whole grain bread when the machine was stopped (unplugged) at the end of the first kneading. About 30 to 40 minutes later the machine may be started over. Testing was successfully done on these machines both ways; it is a matter of your preference.

One pound capacity machines: The specifications for one pound machines are generally 2 cups of bread flour and perhaps up to 2½ cups of a combination of flours or whole grain. The small size recipe would normally be the correct one to use. The motors on all machines are strong enough to knead the dough. The main concern is overflowing the pan.

Each recipe is provided in three sizes so that you may simply select which size is appropriate for your machine or for your needs at the time. Any machine which has a large capacity (1.5 or 2 lbs.) may make a smaller size recipe.

The first ingredient listed in the recipes is always the liquid with yeast being last. For those machines which call for yeast to be used first DAK and Welbilt), simply read the recipes from the bottom up.

Flour equivalents are provided for each recipe so that you may easily judge the correct size recipe to use in your machine or to fit your needs.

RAISIN/MIX CYCLE

Some machines have a separate cycle which has a beep about 5 minutes prior to the end of the second kneading cycle. This beep indicates that raisins, nuts or other similar ingredients should be added. The ingredients which are to be added are found following the line in the recipe. Some machines have a beep on each and every cycle and for those machines, the specific cycle is mentioned. For those machines which do not have a beep, the following guidelines should be used:

National/Panasonic - Add the ingredients following the completion of the first kneading. The machine will indicate that it is during the "REST" period and it is during this time that the yeast is dropped by the dispenser.

Maxim, Chefmate, Mister Loaf, Seiko - Add the ingredients at the beginning along with the remaining ingredients. I generally add the raisins, nuts, etc. in with the liquid ingredients, especially if using the timer.

Quick Baking/Rapid/Turbo cycle - Some machines introduced in the fall of 1992 have specific quick or rapid cycles for whole grains. Testing was not done using these cycles.

Timer - Any recipe using milk, eggs, cheese or other foods which could spoil sitting at room temperature for long periods of time should not be used with the timer. Each recipe indicates whether the timer may or may not be used. The timer is generally not used with a raisin/mix cycle. The exceptions to this are the machines listed above; the ingredients may be added as directed and the timer used if no perishable foods are used.

Setting - Testing of recipes was done on all machines using a medium setting. Sugar darkens the crust; therefore, recipes using a high amount of sugar may be baked using a lighter setting, if available.

NUTRITIONAL INFORMATION

Nutritional information is provided for each recipe based on a 1 oz. slice of bread. The data was compiled using *The Cooking Companion*. Several recipes just call for nonspecific items; we used apple juice concentrate, strawberries for berries, brown rice for rice, 7 grain cereal for any multi-grain, skim milk, and walnuts for nutritional data. All optional ingredients were included; the vital gluten was measured at the lower amount. If two ingredients are listed, for example maple sugar/sucanet, the first ingredient listed is used.

INGREDIENTS AND SUBSTITUTIONS

Fat (butter, margarine, vegetable or nut oils) makes bread tender, gives it a soft crumb and helps to preserve it. Wheat does contain a small amount of fat in both the bran and germ, most of which is washed out during the commercial milling process. Breads made from whole grain flours require less fat in general than loaves made from refined flours.

During the early stages of testing for this book, I experimented with fruit juice concentrates (orange or apple found in the frozen section of the grocery store and thawed for use) as a substitute for sweeteners. What I found, however, was that the amount of fruit juice concentrate required as the sweetener was excessive and began to have a detrimental impact upon the rising of the loaves. I did notice, however, that loaves made with fruit juice concentrate were tender, had a soft crumb and that they seemed to be well preserved.

You may have already heard of replacing fat with applesauce which may be done on a one-to-one basis. The reason applesauce replaces fat is apparently the high amount of pectin, which is a naturally occurring carbohydrate normally used in jelling. It makes sense to me, therefore, that fruit juice concentrates may also replace fat for the same reason: the high pectin. I have done a considerable amount of research and have not found any supporting documentation to my theory — all I can say is that it works!

Fruits which are high in pectin include tart apples, blackberries, cherries, cranberries, grapefruit, grapes, lemons, limes and oranges.

Miso is a fermented soybean paste which is also used to replace fat. However, miso contains salt already so OMIT salt from the recipe. Miso may be purchased at a health food store.

Yeast is the leavening agent used in all of these recipes. The most common type of yeast used is the active dry yeast which is found packaged in three envelopes. This same yeast may be purchased in bulk which is much more economical. If bulk active dry yeast is not available in your grocery store, ask the manager to start carrying it; otherwise it may be ordered through mail order catalogs. Active dry yeast should be used on the regular baking cycle and should never be used on the rapid or quick cycles. The second type of yeast which may be used in machines is quick-rising yeast, sold as RapidRise, QuickRise or SAF-Instant. This yeast must always be used when using the rapid or quick cycle on your machine (not a cake cycle such as on the National/Panasonic or Zojirushi machines). Some people say they use the quick-rising yeast when using their regular, basic cycle and that they prefer the results. You should experiment and see which you prefer with your basic cycle. Fresh or cake yeast is not recommended for use in bread machines.

Salt is one of those necessary "evils" of bread baking. Salt restricts the growth of the yeast and hence the rising of the dough. Without salt, the dough will rise too quickly or too high and then collapse. I have been experimenting with decreasing the salt amounts as much as possible and have successfully used ⅛ tsp. in the small and medium size recipes and ¼ tsp. in the large. For people on a salt-restricted diet, ground dehydrated vegetable flakes (food processor or blender) may be substituted. Check your health food store for a vegetable salt which is used in a 3:1 ratio: for example, if your recipe calls for ⅓ tsp. of salt, use 1 tsp. of vegetable salt.

Sugar or sweeteners are required in bread baking to feed the yeast which enables the dough to rise. Granulated sugars which may be substituted on a basic 1:1 ratio include:

- maple sugar - maple syrup which has been cooked slowly until dried into granules
- date sugar - finely ground dried dates
- sucanet - evaporated sugar cane juice - the only process which it has undergone is the removal of the water. Sucanet contains more nutrients than brown or turbinado sugars
- turbinado sugar - "Raw" sugar which is less refined than white sugar, i.e., not subject to chemical whitening.

Fructose, a natural fruit sugar, is sweeter than sugar so less is needed (rule of thumb is ⅓ the sugar amount). Liquid sweeteners which may be substituted on a 1:1 basis include honey, molasses, barley malt syrup, fruit syrups, maple syrup or rice syrup.

Liquid sweeteners and granulated sweeteners are interchangeable; however, liquid amounts may require adjusting. For example, if a recipe calls for 1 tbs. of sugar and you would prefer to use honey, you may need to delete 1 tbs. of the liquid.

Milk - If a recipe calls for milk but you have an allergy or you would like to use the timer cycle, you may simply substitute water or juice on a cup for cup basis. Nutrition may be boosted by adding dry milk powder in with the flour and other dry ingredients, if desired. Try adding 1 tbs. per cup of flour used. As this is a small percentage of the total dry ingredients no changes are necessary to the liquid or dry amounts. Likewise, if dried milk powder is called for, it may simply be omitted.

Buttermilk substitutes are yogurt, sour cream, 1 tbs. vinegar or lemon juice in bottom of cup and add milk to equal 1 cup.

Eggs assist in providing leavening and add richness, flavor and color to breads. If eggs are called for in a recipe, and you prefer not to use them, just add whatever liquid you are using to compensate for the loss of the egg. A general rule of thumb is ¼ cup of liquid for each whole egg. You should watch the dough and add the liquid as it is kneading until a round ball of dough is formed. Egg substitutes are available in grocery stores: ¼ cup equals one egg. Dry egg powder is available: 1½ tsp. plus 2 tbs. equals one egg. Egg powder may be purchased at a health food store or by mail.

Oats and **wheat flakes** are very similar in appearance and may be used interchangeably. Both are made by rolling the oat groat or wheat kernel; hence they may also be found as rolled oats or wheat. The most commonly known rolled oats are the Quaker oats found at grocery stores. The difference between instant or quick cooking oats and "old fashioned" oats is the thickness; both are acceptable in bread baking.

Chocolate and **unsweetened cocoa** may be replaced with carob chips or carob powder.

Most pumpernickel breads derive coloring from unsweetened cocoa. Several recipes in this book use **black bean flour** which is made in home mills. If you do not have a home mill, you may use **dried black bean flakes** which may be purchased at health food stores or even in some grocery stores. Interchangeable equivalents to cocoa:

black bean flour	¼ cup	⅓ cup	½ cup
black bean flakes	⅓ cup	½ cup	⅔ cup

Cracked wheat is wheat berries which have been cracked or very coarsely ground. Like whole wheat berries, they must be soaked prior to using in a bread recipe. I always soak them a minimum of one hour. In many machines this may be done right in the pan with the other ingredients set on the timer. Just put the cracked wheat in with the liquid and the dry ingredients on top, set the timer and you're off. If baking with a Welbilt, DAK, National or Panasonic machine, simply measure your cracked wheat and the liquid and soak the cracked wheat right in the measuring cup for a minimum of one hour.

Fruit puree is fruit which has simply been liquified in a blender or food processor (steel blade). Fruits all have different moisture contents; keep an eye on the dough and add flour or water as needed to form a nice, round ball of dough.

WHOLE GRAIN WHEAT BREADS

HONEY WHEAT BREAD

This delicious, high-rising, sweet whole grain bread is on the testers' list of favorites. No fat or fat substitutes are used and the honey serves as a natural preservative.

	Small	Medium	Large
water/milk	¾ cup	1⅛ cups	1½ cups
honey	¼ cup	⅓ cup	½ cup
salt	¼ tsp.	⅓ tsp.	½ tsp.
vital gluten, optional	1 to 2 tbs.	1½ to 3 tbs.	2 to 4 tbs.
whole wheat flour	2 cups	3 cups	4 cups
yeast	1½ tsp.	2 tsp.	2½ tsp.

flour equivalents: *2 cups*   *3 cups*   *4 cups*
setting: medium   *timer: yes with water*

Nutritional analysis per 1 oz. slice   75 calories, 0.3 g fat (0.1 g sat fat), 3.2 g protein, 16 g carbohydrate, 0.2 mg cholesterol, 42.8 mg sodium

SOUR CREAM WHEAT BREAD

Four stars for this sandwich bread. The loaf rises moderately high and cuts nicely.

	Small	Medium	Large
sour cream	¾ cup	1⅛ cups	1½ cups
fruit juice concentrate	1 tbs.	2 tbs.	2 tbs.
egg	1	1½	2
sucanet/maple sugar	1 tbs.	1½ tbs.	2 tbs.
salt	¼ tsp.	⅓ tsp.	½ tsp.
baking soda	¼ tsp.	⅓ tsp.	½ tsp.
vital gluten, optional	1 to 2 tbs.	1½ to 3 tbs.	2 to 4 tbs.
whole wheat flour	2 cups	3 cups	4 cups
yeast	1½ tsp.	2 tsp.	2½ tsp.

flour equivalents: *2 cups*   *3 cups*   *4 cups*
setting: medium   *timer: no (sour cream, egg)*

Nutritional analysis per 1 oz. slice   86 calories, 2.9 g fat (1.5 g sat fat), 3.5 g protein, 12.3 g carbohydrate, 18.1 mg cholesterol, 59.1 mg sodium

MAPLE HONEY WHEAT BREAD

A delicious sweet bread which slices well for sandwiches and rises nicely.

	Small	Medium	Large
milk/water	¾ cup	1⅛ cups	1½ cups
fruit juice concentrate	1 tbs.	1½ tbs.	2 tbs.
honey	2 tbs.	3 tbs.	¼ cup
maple syrup	2 tbs.	3 tbs.	¼ cup
salt	¼ tsp.	⅓ tsp.	½ tsp.
vital gluten, optional	1 to 2 tbs.	1½ to 3 tbs.	2 to 4 tbs.
whole wheat flour	2 cups	3 cups	4 cups
yeast	1 tsp.	1½ tsp.	2 tsp.

flour equivalents: *2 cups*   *3 cups*   *4 cups*
setting: light to medium   *timer: yes with water*

Nutritional analysis per 1 oz. slice 71.3 calories, 0.3 g fat (0.1 g sat fat), 3.1 g protein, 14.9 g carbohydrate, 0.2 mg cholesterol, 44.2 mg sodium

WHEAT GERM BREAD

An absolutely superb, dense, sweet whole grain bread. Rises moderately well.

	Small	**Medium**	**Large**
milk/water	⅔ cup	1 cup	1⅓ cups
egg	1	1½	2
fruit juice concentrate	1 tbs.	1½ tbs.	2 tbs.
maple sugar/sucanet	2 tbs.	3 tbs.	¼ cup
salt	¼ tsp.	⅓ tsp.	½ tsp.
cinnamon	¼ tsp.	⅓ tsp.	½ tsp.
nutmeg	⅛ tsp.	⅛+ tsp.	¼ tsp.
vital gluten, optional	1 to 2 tbs.	1½ to 3 tbs.	2 to 4 tbs.
wheat germ	¼ cup	⅓ cup	½ cup
wheat flour	2 cups	3 cups	4 cups
yeast	1½ tsp.	2 tsp.	2½ tsp.

flour equivalents: 2¼ cups   3⅓ cups   4½ cups
setting: medium   *timer: no (milk, eggs)*

Nutritional analysis per 1 oz. slice   112 calories, 1.9 g fat (0.6 g sat fat), 7.4 g protein, 18 g carbohydrate, 13.5 mg cholesterol, 45.8 mg sodium

HONEY PEASANT BREAD

A moist, chewy bread with a light, crispy crust. Few ingredients make this a quick and easy bread with a moderate rise.

	Small	Medium	Large
water	1 cup	1½ cups	2 cups
honey	1 tsp.	1½ tsp.	2 tsp.
salt	¼ tsp.	⅓ tsp.	½ tsp.
vital gluten, optional	1 to 2 tbs.	1½ to 3 tbs.	2 to 4 tbs.
___ flour	2 cups	3 cups	4 cups
		1½ tsp.	2 tsp.

flour equivalents: 4 cups
setting: medium   timer: yes

Nutritional analysis per 1 oz. slice   55.9 calories, 0.3 g fat (0.0 g sat fat), 2.7 g protein, 11.3 g carbohydrate, 0.0 mg cholesterol, 73 mg sodium

WHOLE GRAIN PEASANT BREAD

An earthy, nutty moist bread with an open texture. As with any peasant bread, the high liquid to flour ratio may result in a concave top.

	Small	Medium	Large
water	1 cup	1½ cups	2 cups
maple/date sugar	1 tsp.	1½ tsp.	2 tsp.
salt	¼ tsp.	⅓ tsp.	½ tsp.
vital gluten, optional	1 to 2 tbs.	1½ to 3 tbs.	2 to 4 tbs.
whole wheat flour	2 cups	3 cups	4 cups
yeast	1 tsp.	1½ tsp.	2 tsp.

flour equivalents: *2 cups*   *3 cups*   *4 cups*
setting: medium   *timer: yes*

Nutritional analysis per 1 oz. slice   55.6 calories, 0.3 g fat (0.0 g sat fat), 2.7 g protein, 11.3 g carbohydrate, 0.0 mg cholesterol, 48.9 mg sodium

BASIC SOUR CREAM BREAD

A great sandwich bread! It is also good with a spicy soup and/or salad. Rises and slices nicely.

	Small	Medium	Large
sour cream	1 cup	1½ cups	2 cups
maple sugar/sucanet	1½ tsp.	2¼ tsp.	1 tbs.
salt	¼ tsp.	⅓ tsp.	½ tsp.
baking soda	¼ tsp.	⅓ tsp.	½ tsp.
vital gluten, optional	1 to 2 tbs.	1½ to 3 tbs.	2 to 4 tbs.
whole wheat flour	2 cups	3 cups	4 cups
yeast	1 tsp.	1½ tsp.	2 tsp.

flour equivalents: *2 cups*   *3 cups*   *4 cups*
setting: medium   *timer: no (sour cream)*

Nutritional analysis per 1 oz. slice   86.8 calories, 3.3 g fat (1.9 g sat fat), 3.2 g protein, 12 g carbohydrate, 6.4 mg cholesterol, 93 mg sodium

CRACKED WHEAT BREAD

A terrific crunchy bread. The cracked wheat must soak in the liquid at least one hour (see page 21). Moderate rise.

	Small	Medium	Large
water	¾ cup	1⅛ cups	1½ cups
cracked wheat	⅓ cup	½ cup	⅔ cups
vegetable oil	1 tbs.	1½ tbs.	2 tbs.
honey	1 tbs.	1½ tbs.	2 tbs.
salt	¼ tsp.	⅓ tsp.	½ tsp.
vital gluten, optional	1 to 2 tbs.	1½ to 3 tbs.	2 to 4 tbs.
whole wheat flour	1⅔ cups	2½ cups	3⅓ cups
yeast	1 tsp.	1½ tsp.	2 tsp.

flour equivalents: *2 cups*   *3 cups*   *4 cups*
setting: medium   *timer: yes*

Nutritional analysis per 1 oz. slice   66.2 calories, 1.1 g fat (0.2 g sat fat), 2.7 g protein, 12.2 g carbohydrate, 0.0 mg cholesterol, 73.3 mg sodium

ENGLISH MUFFIN BREAD ✗✗

This is an adaptation to whole grain of one of our favorite recipes. A relatively high liquid amount gives this bread an open grain texture. Sunken tops may result but the taste is really worth that risk!

	Small	**Medium**	**Large**
water/milk	1 cup	1½ cups	2 cups
maple/date sugar	1½ tsp.	2¼ tsp.	1 tbs.
salt	¼ tsp.	⅓ tsp.	½ tsp.
baking soda	⅛ tsp.	⅛+ tsp.	¼ tsp.
whole wheat flour	2 cups	3 cups	4 cups
vital gluten, optional	1 to 2 tbs.	1½ to 3 tbs.	2 to 4 tbs.
yeast	1 tsp.	1½ tsp.	2 tsp.

flour equivalents: *2 cups*   *3 cups*   *4 cups*
setting: medium   *timer: yes with water*

Nutritional analysis per 1 oz. slice 61.4 calories, 0.3 g fat (0.1 g sat fat), 3.3 g protein, 12.1 g carbohydrate, 0.3 mg cholesterol, 57.3 mg sodium

BASIC BUTTERMILK WHEAT

A great basic wheat bread which is good for sandwiches or toast. A medium-rising loaf.

	Small	Medium	Large
buttermilk	¾ cup	1⅛ cups	1½ cups
fruit juice concentrate	1 tbs.	1½ tbs.	2 tbs.
maple/brown sugar	2 tbs.	3 tbs.	¼ cup
salt	¼ tsp.	⅓ tsp.	½ tsp.
baking soda	¼ tsp.	⅓ tsp.	½ tsp.
vital gluten, optional	1 to 2 tbs.	1½ to 3 tbs.	2 to 4 tbs.
whole wheat flour	2 cups	3 cups	4 cups
yeast	1 tsp.	1½ tsp.	2 tsp.

flour equivalents: *2 cups*   *3 cups*   *4 cups*
setting: medium   *timer: no (buttermilk)*

Nutritional analysis per 1 oz. slice   61.2 calories, 0.4 g fat (0.1 g sat fat), 3.1 g protein, 12 g carbohydrate, 0.4 mg cholesterol, 61.4 mg sodium

YOGURT WHEAT BREAD

★★ Yogurt takes longer to knead so start the machine over again after 10-15 min.

I use plain nonfat yogurt in this recipe. A fruited yogurt would add extra flavor and would be great too. This is a low-rising, densely textured, delicious bread.

	Small	Medium	Large
egg	1		
yogurt	3/4 cup	1⅛ cups	1½ cups
fruit juice concentrate	1 tbs.	1½ tbs.	2 tbs.
honey	2 tbs.	3 tbs.	4 tbs.
salt	¼ tsp.	⅓ tsp.	½ tsp.
vital gluten, optional	1 to 2 tbs.	1½ to 3 tbs.	2 to 4 tbs.
whole wheat flour	2 cups	3 cups	4 cups
yeast	1 tsp.	1½ tsp.	2 tsp.

flour equivalents:	*2 cups*	*3 cups*	*4 cups*
setting: medium	*timer: no (yogurt)*		

Nutritional analysis per 1 oz. slice   69.8 calories, 0.4 g fat (0.1 g sat fat), 3.3 g protein, 14 g carbohydrate, 0.7 mg cholesterol, 80.1 mg sodium

WHEAT FLAKE BREAD

Wheat flakes are rolled and are similar to in appearance to rolled oats (Quaker oats) and give this bread great taste and texture.

	Small	Medium	Large
water/milk	¾ cup	1⅛ cups	1½ cups
honey	2 tbs.	3 tbs.	¼ cup
salt	¼ tsp.	⅓ tsp.	½ tsp.
vital gluten, optional	1 to 2 tbs.	1½ to 3 tbs.	2 to 4 tbs.
rolled wheat flakes	½ cup	¾ cup	1 cup
whole wheat flour	1½ cups	2¼ cups	3 cups
yeast	1 tsp.	1½ tsp.	2 tsp.

flour equivalents:	*2 cups*	*3 cups*	*4 cups*
setting: medium	*timer: yes with water*		

Nutritional analysis per 1 oz. slice 80.7 calories, 0.4 g fat (0.0 g sat fat), 3.6 g protein, 16.4 g carbohydrate, 0.2 mg cholesterol, 42.7 mg sodium

BRAN BREAD

Using bran usually results in a denser loaf of bread. This loaf has a moist, even texture and rises moderately.

	Small	Medium	Large
egg	1		
water/milk	¾ cup	1⅛ cups	1½ cups
fruit juice concentrate	1½ tbs.	2⅓ tbs.	3 tbs.
honey/maple syrup	2 tbs.	3 tbs.	4 tbs.
salt	¼ tsp.	⅓ tsp.	½ tsp.
baking soda	½ tsp.	¾ tsp.	1 tsp.
wheat/oat bran	⅓ cup	½ cup	⅔ cup
vital gluten, optional	1 to 2 tbs.	1½ to 3 tbs.	2 to 4 tbs.
whole wheat flour	2 cups	3 cups	4 cups
yeast	1 tsp.	1½ tsp.	2 tsp.

flour equivalents: 2⅓ cups   3½ cups   4⅔ cups
setting: medium   *timer: yes with water*

Nutritional analysis per 1 oz. slice   72.4 calories, 0.5 g fat (0.1 g sat fat), 3.5 g protein, 14.3 g carbohydrate, 0.2 mg cholesterol, 69.8 mg sodium

WHEAT GERM SESAME BREAD

The combination of wheat germ and sesame seeds is a great flavor enhancer and also contributes to this being a heavy textured, low-rising loaf of bread.

	Small	Medium	Large
apple juice	⅞ cup	1¼ cups	1¾ cups
honey/maple syrup	2 tbs.	3 tbs.	4 tbs.
salt	¼ tsp.	⅓ tsp.	½ tsp.
baking soda	½ tsp.	¾ tsp.	1 tsp.
wheat germ	¼ cup	⅓ cup	½ cup
sesame seeds	2 tbs.	3 tbs.	¼ cup
vital gluten, optional	1 to 2 tbs.	1½ to 3 tbs.	2 to 4 tbs.
whole wheat flour	2 cups	3 cups	4 cups
yeast	1½ tsp.	2 tsp.	2½ tsp.
flour equivalents:	*2⅓ cups*	*3½ cups*	*4¾ cups*
setting: medium	*timer: yes*		

Nutritional analysis per 1 oz. slice 167 calories, 3.3 g fat (1 g sat fat), 11.7 g protein, 26.3 g carbohydrate, 0.0 mg cholesterol, 64.2 mg sodium

HONEY WHEAT BERRY BREAD

This is well worth the effort. Watch the moisture of the dough (see page 7).

	Small	Medium	Large
soaked berries:			
wheat berries	⅓ cup	½ cup	⅔ cup
water	1 cup	1½ cups	2 cups
honey	2 tbs.	3 tbs.	¼ cup

Combine ingredients in a saucepan and bring to a rolling boil for about 5 minutes, stirring occasionally. Cover the pan and remove from heat and let sit for 6 to 12 hours or overnight. Drain any standing water before adding the berries to remaining ingredients.

	Small	Medium	Large
water	¾ cup	1⅛ cups	1½ cups
honey	2 tbs.	3 tbs.	4 tbs.
salt	⅓ tsp.	½ tsp.	⅔ tsp.
vital gluten, optional	1 to 2 tbs.	1½ to 3 tbs.	2 to 4 tbs.
wheat flour	2 cups	3 cups	4 cups
yeast	1 tsp.	1½ tsp.	2 tsp.
flour equivalents:	2⅓ cups	3½ cups	4⅔ cups
setting: medium	*timer: yes*		

Nutritional analysis per 1 oz. slice 84.2 calories, 0.4 g fat (0.0 g sat fat), 3.3 g protein, 18.3 g carbohydrate, 0.0 mg cholesterol, 37.7 mg sodium

BUTTERMILK HONEY BREAD

Both buttermilk and egg yolks have "magical" leavening effects on bread. You'll love this if you like a lighter, airier whole grain bread.

	Small	Medium	Large
buttermilk	¾ cup	1⅛ cups	1½ cups
egg	1	1½	2
fruit juice concentrate	1 tbs.	1⅓ tbs.	1½ tbs.
honey	2 tbs.	2½ tbs.	3 tbs.
salt	¾ tsp.	1 tsp.	1½ tsp.
vital gluten, optional	1 to 2 tbs.	1½ to 3 tbs.	2 to 4 tbs.
baking soda	¼ tsp.	⅓ tsp.	½ tsp.
whole wheat flour	2¼ cups	3⅓ cups	4½ cups
yeast	1 tsp.	1½ tsp.	2 tsp.

flour equivalents: *2¼ cups*   *3⅓ cups*   *4½ cups*
setting: medium   *timer: no (buttermilk, eggs)*

Nutritional analysis per 1 oz. slice   78.6 calories, 0.7 g fat (0.2 g sat fat), 3.8 g protein, 15.1 g carbohydrate, 13.7 mg cholesterol, 65.6 mg sodium

CREAMY BUTTERMILK WHEAT BREAD

An outstanding bread. Evaporated skim milk may replace the heavy cream if desired. Rises nicely due to both egg and buttermilk.

	Small	Medium	Large
buttermilk	1/2 cup	3/4 cup	1 cup
heavy cream	2½ tbs.	1/4 cup	1/3 cup
fruit juice concentrate	2 tbs.	3 tbs.	4 tbs.
egg	1	1½	2
honey	1 tbs.	1½ tbs.	2 tbs.
salt	1/4 tsp.	1/3 tsp.	1/2 tsp.
vital gluten, optional	1 to 2 tbs.	1½ to 3 tbs.	2 to 4 tbs.
baking soda	1/4 tsp.	1/3 tsp.	1/2 tsp.
whole wheat flour	2¼ cups	3⅓ cups	4½ cups
yeast	1½ tsp.	2 tsp.	2½ tsp.

flour equivalents: *2¼ cups*   *3⅓ cups*   *4½ cups*
setting: medium   *timer: no (buttermilk, cream, egg)*

Nutritional analysis per 1 oz. slice 81.8 calories, 1.6 g fat (0.8 g sat fat), 3.7 g protein, 13.9 g carbohydrate, 17 mg cholesterol, 62.4 mg sodium

MAPLE WHEAT FLAKES BREAD

Wheat flakes are rolled and are similar in appearance to rolled oats, which may also be used. Wonderful maple flavor. Use fruit juice concentrate in place of the oil if desired.

	Small	**Medium**	**Large**
water/milk	¾ cup	1⅛ cups	1½ cups
vegetable oil	2 tsp.	1 tbs.	1⅓ tbs.
maple syrup	2 tbs.	3 tbs.	¼ cup
salt	⅓ tsp.	½ tsp.	⅔ tsp.
baking soda	½ tsp.	¾ tsp.	1 tsp.
vital gluten, optional	1 to 2 tbs.	1½ to 3 tbs.	2 to 4 tbs.
wheat flakes	½ cup	¾ cup	1 cup
whole wheat flour	2 cups	3 cups	4 cups
yeast	1 tsp.	1½ tsp.	2 tsp.

flour equivalents: 2½ cups   3¾ cups   5 cups
setting: medium   *timer: yes with water*

Nutritional analysis per 1 oz. slice   96.6 calories, 1 g fat (0.1 g sat fat), 4.1 g protein, 18.5 g carbohydrate, 0.2 mg cholesterol, 70 mg sodium

SPROUT BREADS AND SOURDOUGH BREADS

Breads made with sprouts or with a sourdough starter are combined in this section because they require advance planning. Both have variables which can alter the liquid/flour ratio. It is extremely IMPORTANT that you watch the dough ball. Allow the dough to knead for approximately 5 minutes and then check it. Add water or flour one tablespoon at a time as the dough is kneading until a round ball of dough is achieved.

Sprouting wheat berries, other grains or beans and using them in bread is a great way to increase both the flavor and nutrition. The seeds, grains or beans begin to germinate and grow. During this process the seeds eat their own starch which increases the overall protein and vitamin content and lowers the carbohydrates and the calories.

Always use fresh, unbroken seeds or beans for sprouting and never use any seeds which have been sprayed with fungicides. If you purchase your seeds or beans through reputable food sources, they should be okay. Pearled barley has had the outer husk of the grain removed and will not sprout; whole barley which is what is needed to sprout is more difficult to locate.

HOW TO SPROUT

There are special sprouter jars or kits available for purchase at most health food stores or through many mail order catalogs. While they are very nice, a clear glass jar and some cheesecloth fastened to the jar with a rubber band does just fine! Fill the jar approximately ¼ of the way with your seeds or beans and rinse a few times. Fill the jar with water and allow to sit overnight or for at least 8 to 12 hours. Drain and rinse again, right through the cheesecloth or the wire screen lid. Set the jar, mouth side down, at a 45° angle in a warm, dark place (I put it in a dark corner or in a cupboard). Rinse the sprouts once or twice a day.

Any sprouts may be used in place of the sprouted wheat berries. Experiment and have fun! Various seeds/beans/grains which may be sprouted and used in bread baking include:

	DAYS TO HARVEST	LENGTH OF SPROUT
amaranth	2 to 3	¼ inch
barley	3 to 4	length of seed
chickpeas/garbanzo/soybeans	2 to 4	¾ to 1¼ inch
lentils/black beans/cranberry beans	3 to 4	½ to 1 inch
rye/wheat berries	3 to 4	length of seed
kashi-breakfast pilaf	3 to 4	length of seed

Leftover sprouts may be refrigerated in plastic or glass bowls or containers for one to three days. Add to cereal, cottage cheese, tuna or chicken salads, green salads or to sandwiches.

Sprout bread tends to be a little denser and lower rising than "normal" and has lots of flavor. The sprouts count towards the flour equivalents.

SPROUTED WHEAT BREAD

A wonderful loaf of nutritious bread which rises to a medium height. An egg in the bottom of the water/milk measuring cup assists in increasing the height if desired. Watch the dough for moisture (see pages 13 and 14).

	Small	Medium	Large
water/milk	2/3 cup	1 cup	1 1/3 cups
fruit juice concentrate	1 tbs.	1 1/2 tbs.	2 tbs.
honey	1 tbs.	1 1/2 tbs.	2 tbs.
sprouted wheat berries	1/3 cup	1/2 cup	2/3 cup
salt	1/4 tsp.	1/3 tsp.	1/2 tsp.
whole wheat flour	2 cups	3 cups	4 cups
vital gluten, optional	1 to 2 tbs.	1 1/2 to 3 tbs.	2 to 4 tbs.
yeast	1 tsp.	1 1/2 tsp.	2 tsp.
flour equivalents:	*2 1/3 cups*	*3 1/2 cups*	*4 2/3 cups*
setting: medium	*timer: yes with water*		

Nutritional analysis per 1 oz. slice 60.8 calories, 0.3 g fat (0.0 g sat fat), 2.8 g protein, 12.6 g carbohydrate, 0.0 mg cholesterol, 36.9 mg sodium

SPROUTED WHEAT MULTI-GRAIN BREAD

This great multi-grain bread rises to a medium height. Watch the dough for moisture (see pages 13 and 14).

	Small	**Medium**	**Large**
water/milk	⅔ cup	1 cup	1⅓ cups
egg	½	1	1
honey	2 tbs.	3 tbs.	¼ cup
sprouted wheat berries	⅓ cup	½ cup	⅔ cup
salt	¼ tsp.	⅓ tsp.	½ tsp.
baking soda	½ tsp.	¾ tsp.	1 tsp.
7 or 9 grain cereal	½ cup	¾ cup	1 cup
whole wheat flour	1¾ cups	2⅔ cups	3½ cups
vital gluten, optional	1 to 2 tbs.	1½ to 3 tbs.	2 to 4 tbs.
yeast	1 tsp.	1½ tsp.	2 tsp.
flour equivalents:	*2½ cups*	*3¾ cups*	*5 cups*
setting: medium	*timer: no (egg)*		

Nutritional analysis per 1 oz. slice   85.7 calories, 0.7 g fat (0.0 g sat fat), 3.8 g protein, 16.6 g carbohydrate, 6.7 mg cholesterol, 64.8 mg sodium

SPROUTED BEAN BREAD

*Sprout any dried bean, such as black, cranberry, navy or lima for this nutritious bread. See **How to Sprout**, page 42. Watch the dough for moisture (see pages 13 and 14).*

	Small	**Medium**	**Large**
buttermilk	¾ cup	1⅛ cups	1½ cups
egg	1	1½	2
sprouted beans	½ cup	¾ cup	1 cup
maple sugar/sucanet	2 tbs.	3 tbs.	¼ cup
salt	½ tsp.	¾ tsp.	1 tsp.
baking soda	⅓ tsp.	½ tsp.	⅔ tsp.
vital gluten, optional	1 to 2 tbs.	1½ to 3 tbs.	2 to 4 tbs.
whole wheat flour	2¼ cups	3⅓ cups	4½ cups
yeast	1½ tsp.	2 tsp.	2½ tsp.

flour equivalents: *2¾ cups*   *4+ cups*   *5½ cups*
setting: medium   *timer: no (buttermilk, egg)*

Nutritional analysis per 1 oz. slice   77.7 calories, 0.8 g fat (0.2 g sat fat), 3.9 g protein, 14.7 g carbohydrate, 13.7 mg cholesterol, 81.8 mg sodium

SPROUTED KASHI PILAF

Make sure you purchase the "kashi breakfast pilaf" for sprouting as it is really a combination of sproutable berries and seeds. Watch the moisture of the dough and scrape the sides of the pan if necessary (see pages 13 and 14).

	Small	**Medium**	**Large**
water/milk	¾ cup	1⅛ cups	1½ cups
fruit juice concentrate	2 tsp.	1 tbs.	1⅓ tbs.
honey	1 tbs.	1½ tbs.	2 tbs.
sprouted kashi	⅓ cup	½ cup	⅔ cup
baking soda	½ tsp.	¾ tsp.	1 tsp.
salt	¼ tsp.	⅓ tsp.	½ tsp.
whole wheat flour	2 cups	3 cups	4 cups
vital gluten, optional	1 to 2 tbs.	1½ to 3 tbs.	2 to 4 tbs.
yeast	1 tsp.	1½ tsp.	2 tsp.
flour equivalents:	*2⅓ cups*	*3½ cups*	*4⅔ cups*
setting: medium	*timer: yes*		

Nutritional analysis per 1 oz. slice 68.2 calories, 0.3 g fat (0.0 g sat fat), 3.0 g protein, 14.3 g carbohydrate, 0.0 mg cholesterol, 62.9 mg sodium

SPROUTED SOY BREAD

A great source of protein, soy really adds both nutrition and flavor to this bread. For information on miso, see page 17. Watch the moisture (see pages 13 and 14).

	Small	Medium	Large
water/milk	⅔ cup	1 cup	1⅓ cups
miso	1 tbs.	1½ tbs.	2 tbs.
honey	2 tbs.	3 tbs.	4 tbs.
sprouted soy beans	⅓ cup	½ cup	⅔ cup
baking soda	½ tsp.	¾ tsp.	1 tsp.
whole wheat flour	2 cups	3 cups	4 cups
vital gluten, optional	1 to 2 tbs.	1½ to 3 tbs.	2 to 4 tbs.
yeast	1 tsp.	1½ tsp.	2 tsp.

flour equivalents:	*2⅓ cups*	*3½ cups*	*4⅔ cups*
setting: medium	*timer: yes with water*		

Nutritional analysis per 1 oz. slice   67.0 calories, 0.4 g fat (0 g sat fat), 3.1 g protein, 13.8 g carbohydrate, 0 mg cholesterol, 135 mg sodium

YOGURT SPROUTED BREAD

*This is wonderful. Buttermilk or sour cream could be substituted for the yogurt if desired. See **buttermilk**, page 20. Watch the dough for moisture (see pages 13 and 14).*

	Small	**Medium**	**Large**
water	2 tbs.	3 tbs.	¼ cup
yogurt	¾ cup	1⅛ cups	1½ cups
honey	2 tbs.	3 tbs.	¼ cup
sprouted wheat berries	⅓ cup	½ cup	⅔ cup
baking soda	½ tsp.	¾ tsp.	1 tsp.
salt	¼ tsp.	⅓ tsp.	½ tsp.
vital gluten, optional	1 to 2 tbs.	1½ to 3 tbs.	2 to 4 tbs.
wheat flour	2 cups	3 cups	4 cups
yeast	1½ tsp.	2 tsp.	2½ tsp.
flour equivalents:	*2⅓ cups*	*3½ cups*	*4⅔ cups*
setting: medium	*timer: no (yogurt)*		

Nutritional analysis per 1 oz. slice   71.5 calories, 0.5 g fat (0.1 g sat fat), 3.4 g protein, 14.4 g carbohydrate, 0.7 mg cholesterol, 69.9 mg sodium

ABOUT SOURDOUGH

A sourdough starter is nothing more than a flour and milk or water mixture which sits at room temperature for several days and catches live yeast bacteria from the air. Today, most starters use yeast in the original starter or in the bread recipe itself — or both. After much experimenting with sourdoughs in bread machines, I recommend also using yeast in the recipes as it helps to maintain the flavor of the sourdough itself but also assists in a higher rising loaf of bread.

A starter may either be purchased or made yourself. To make your own starter, mix together in a glass or plastic bowl:

> 2 cups lukewarm water or milk (110°-115°)
> 2 cups whole wheat bread flour
> 2½ tsp. (1 pkg.) yeast

Cover the bowl and allow to sit in a warm, draft-free location for 4 to 7 days, gently stirring once a day. You may notice that the mixture bubbles and may even overflow the bowl; this is an indication of the fermentation going on. It is also common for the starter to bubble up and then collapse if moved or jarred somehow. A sour smelling liquid may form on top of the starter which may simply be stirred back into the starter prior to use. It is generally recommended that you stir your starter with a wooden or plastic spoon. After the starter has had a chance to "mature," it will form the liquid on top and/or bubble, it may be refrigerated.

FEEDING AND USING STARTER

If the starter is refrigerated, remove it 12 to 24 hours in advance so that it is brought up to room temperature. Simply remove the amount of starter called for in the recipe and add to the other ingredients. Replace the amount removed with equal amounts of water/milk and whole wheat (bread) flour. For example, if 1 cup of starter is used in your recipe, stir one cup of water and one cup of flour back into the mixture; this is called "feeding" your starter. Allow the starter to sit in a warm, draft-free location for approximately 24 hours after which time it may be used again or refrigerated. If using purchased starter, it is usually considered free of any white or refined flour after three feedings.

A starter must be used at least once a week or remove a portion (usually one cup) and throw that away. Feed as usual. If this is not done, your starter will become rancid as it requires fresh flour to feed on. Should you be away from your starter, freeze it and then thaw it in the refrigerator upon your return. As soon as it is thawed, it may be fed as above. The longer the starter is used, the stronger it becomes in flavor.

IMPORTANT!

Sourdough starters develop their own personalities and flavors; some may be thicker than others depending on variables such as the type of flour or the liquid used. For this reason it is imperative to watch the dough as it kneads. I recommend that you allow the machine to knead the dough for approximately 3 to 5 minutes and then check it to see if it has formed a nice round dough ball. If not, add a tablespoon of water or flour at a time until it does so. You may even want to keep notes if necessary. Once you have a good "feel" for whether you need to add more water or flour than the recipes call for, you could begin to use the timer cycle with your changes already made. Sourdough breads usually have very long rising times; therefore I recommend using the longest cycle available on your machine and I always use a medium setting.

WHOLE GRAIN SOURDOUGH

Perfect! One of our favorites. A medium-rising loaf with a thin crust.

	Small	Medium	Large
starter	¾ cup	1⅛ cups	1½ cups
milk/water	¼ cup	⅓ cup	½ cup
vegetable oil	1 tbs.	1½ tbs.	2 tbs.
honey or molasses	2 tbs.	3 tbs.	¼ cup
salt	¼ tsp.	⅓ tsp.	½ tsp.
whole wheat flour	2 cups	3 cups	4 cups
vital gluten, optional	1 tbs.	1½ tbs.	2 tbs.
yeast	1 tsp.	1½ tsp.	2 tsp.

flour equivalents:	*2⅓ cups*	*3½ cups*	*4 cups*
setting: medium	*timer: no (milk)*		

Nutritional analysis per 1 oz. slice 86.8 calories, 1.2 g fat (0.2 g sat fat), 2.9 g protein, 17.3 g carbohydrate, 0.1 mg cholesterol, 38.8 mg sodium

SOURDOUGH ONION BREAD

Onion gives this sourdough a real twist — terrific.

	Small	Medium	Large
starter	⅔ cup	1 cup	1⅓ cups
milk	⅓ cup	½ cup	⅔ cup
diced onions	¼ cup	⅓ cup	½ cup
brown sugar	1 tbs.	1½ tbs.	2 tbs.
salt	⅓ tsp.	½ tsp.	⅔ tsp.
whole wheat flour	2 cups	3 cups	4 cups
vital gluten, optional	1 tbs.	1½ tbs.	2 tbs.
yeast	1 tsp.	1½ tsp.	2 tsp.

flour equivalents: *2 cups*   *3 cups*   *4 cups*
setting: medium   *timer: no (milk)*

Nutritional analysis per 1 oz. slice   66.8 calories, 0.3 g fat (0.1 g sat fat), 2.9 g protein, 13.8 g carbohydrate, 0.1 mg cholesterol, 51.6 mg sodium

SOURDOUGH ONION RYE

This is out of this world. As with any rye, this tends to be low-rising.

	Small	Medium	Large
starter	½ cup	¾ cup	1 cup
water/milk	½ cup	¾ cup	1 cup
diced onion	¼ cup	⅓ cup	½ cup
fruit juice concentrate	1 tbs.	1½ tbs.	2 tbs.
molasses/honey	2 tbs.	3 tbs.	¼ cup
salt	½ tsp.	¾ tsp.	1 tsp.
anise/caraway, optional	2 tsp.	1 tbs.	1⅓ tbs.
vital gluten	1 to 2 tbs.	1½ to 3 tbs.	2 to 4 tbs.
rye flour	½ cup	¾ cup	1 cup
whole wheat flour	2 cups	3 cups	4 cups
yeast	1 tsp.	1½ tsp.	2 tsp.

flour equivalents: 2¾ *cups*   4½ *cups*   5½ *cups*
setting: medium   *timer: yes with water*

Nutritional analysis per 1 oz. slice   78.9 calories, 0.4 g fat (0.0 g sat fat), 3.4 g protein, 16.3 g carbohydrate, 0.0 mg cholesterol, 75.4 mg sodium

SOURDOUGH PUMPERNICKEL

Outstanding! The cocoa provides color for this bread. Low to medium rise.

	Small	Medium	Large
starter	½ cup	¾ cup	1 cup
water	½ cup	¾ cup	1 cup
vegetable oil	1 tbs.	1½ tbs.	2 tbs.
molasses	2 tbs.	3 tbs.	¼ cup
unsweetened cocoa	1 tbs.	1½ tbs.	2 tbs.
salt	½ tsp.	¾ tsp.	1 tsp.
caraway seeds, optional	2 tsp.	1 tbs.	1⅓ tbs.
rye flour	½ cup	¾ cup	1 cup
vital gluten, optional	1 to 2 tbs.	1½ to 3 tbs.	2 to 4 tbs.
whole wheat flour	1¾ cups	2⅓ cups	3½ cups
yeast	1½ tsp.	2 tsp.	2½ tsp.

flour equivalents: *2½ cups*   *3¾ cups*   *5 cups*
setting: medium   *timer: yes*

Nutritional analysis per 1 oz. slice   80 calories, 1.2 g fat (0.2 g sat fat), 3.2 g protein, 15 g carbohydrate, 0.1 mg cholesterol, 77.5 mg sodium

SOURDOUGH MAPLE WALNUT BREAD

A twist on a basic sourdough. Rises to approximately 3⁄4 of the pan.

	Small	**Medium**	**Large**
starter	1⁄2 cup	3⁄4 cup	1 cup
milk/water	1⁄3 cup	1⁄2 cup	2⁄3 cup
maple syrup	2 tbs.	3 tbs.	1⁄4 cup
egg	1	11⁄2	2
cinnamon, optional	1⁄4 tsp.	1⁄3 tsp.	1⁄2 tsp.
salt	1⁄3 tsp.	1⁄2 tsp.	2⁄3 tsp.
vital gluten, optional	1 to 2 tbs.	11⁄2 to 3 tbs.	2 to 4 tbs.
whole wheat flour	21⁄2 cups	31⁄3 cups	41⁄2 cups
yeast	1 tsp.	11⁄2 tsp.	2 tsp.
———			
chopped walnuts	1⁄4 cup	1⁄3 cup	1⁄2 cup
raisins, optional	1⁄4 cup	1⁄3 cup	1⁄2 cup

flour equivalents: *23⁄4 cups*   *41⁄2 cups*   *51⁄2 cups*
setting: medium   *timer: no (milk, egg)*

Nutritional analysis per 1 oz. slice   105 calories, 1.8 g fat (0.2 g sat fat), 4.6 g protein, 18.9 g carbohydrate, 13.4 mg cholesterol, 57.2 mg sodium

REFRIGERATED SOURDOUGH

Wow! An easy way to get that sourdough taste without the standard starter. The starter is very moist and sticky when removing it from the pan to refrigerate.

	Small	Medium	Large
starter*			
water (100° to 110°)	½ cup	¾ cup	1 cup
whole wheat flour	1 cup	1½ cups	2 cups
vital gluten	1 tsp.	1½ tsp.	2 tsp.
yeast	1½ tsp.	2 tsp.	2½ tsp.

Place in machine (any cycle) as usual and allow to knead for 5 to 10 minutes. (Stop machine at that time by using your "stop" or "reset" button or by unplugging.) Dough will be very soft and sticky. Remove from pan and place in a glass bowl, cover with plastic and refrigerate overnight (6 hours to a day and a half). Bring to room temperature prior to starting machine.

dough

starter	*	*	*
water	⅓ cup +/	½ cup+/	⅔ cup +/
fruit juice concentrate	1 tbs.	1½ tbs.	2 tbs.
date/maple sugar	1 tsp.	1½ tsp.	2 tsp.
salt	⅓ tsp.	½ tsp.	⅔ tsp.
whole wheat flour	1 cup	1½ cups	2 cups
vital gluten, optional	1 to 2 tbs.	1½ to 3 tbs.	2 to 4 tbs.

This dough needs to be watched and more water added if necessary. Start with the amount called for and add more 1 tbs. at a time until a soft, round ball is formed.

flour equivalents:	*2 cups*	*3 cups*	*4 cups*
setting: medium	*timer: yes*		

Nutritional analysis per 1 oz. slice   56.7 calories, 0.3 g fat (0.0 g sat fat), 2.9 g protein, 11.3 g carbohydrate, 0.0 mg cholesterol, 49 mg sodium.

MULTI-GRAIN BREADS

OAT WHEAT BREAD

A low- to medium-rising, densely textured loaf with a delicious taste, this makes great toast or French toast.

	Small	**Medium**	**Large**
water/milk	¾ cup	1⅛ cups	1½ cups
applesauce	2 tbs.	3 tbs.	¼ cup
honey	1 tbs.	1½ tbs.	2 tbs.
salt	¼ tsp.	⅓ tsp.	½ tsp.
oats	½ cup	¾ cup	1 cup
oat/wheat bran	2 tbs.	3 tbs.	¼ cup
vital gluten, optional	1 to 2 tbs.	1½ to 3 tbs.	2 to 4 tbs.
whole wheat flour	1½ cups	2¼ cups	3 cups
yeast	1½ tsp.	2 tsp.	2½ tsp.

flour equivalents: *2⅛ cups*   *3¼ cups*   *4¼ cups*
setting: medium   *timer: yes with water*

Nutritional analysis per 1 oz. slice   59.6 calories, 0.5 g fat (0.1 g sat fat), 2.8 g protein, 11.8 g carbohydrate, 0.0 mg cholesterol, 37 mg sodium

POTATO RYE

A wonderful bread which combines two favorites. Make sure the potato is loosely packed in the cup.

	Small	Medium	Large
mashed potato	½ cup	¾ cup	1 cup
potato water	½ cup	¾ cup	1 cup
vegetable oil	1 tbs.	1½ tbs.	2 tbs.
honey/molasses	1 tbs.	1½ tbs.	2 tbs.
salt	¼ to ½ tsp.	⅓ to ¾ tsp.	½ to 1 tsp.
vital gluten, optional	1 to 2 tbs.	1½ to 3 tbs.	2 to 4 tbs.
caraway seeds, optional	1 tsp.	1½ tsp.	2 tsp.
rye flour	½ cup	¾ cup	1 cup
whole wheat flour	1½ cups	2¼ cups	3 cups
yeast	1 tsp.	1½ tsp.	2 tsp.
flour equivalents:	*2 cups*	*3 cups*	*4 cups*

setting: medium   *timer: yes*

Nutritional analysis per 1 oz. slice   71.7 calories, 1.4 g fat (0.2 g sat fat), 2.8 g protein, 13 g carbohydrate, 0.1 mg cholesterol, 56.4 mg sodium

POTATO MULTI-GRAIN BREAD

Use any 4, 7, 9 or 12 grain cereal for this easy, delicious bread. The potato should be loosely packed in the cup. Watch moisture — and sides of pan may require scraping due to potato.

	Small	Medium	Large
mashed potato	½ cup	¾ cup	1 cup
potato water	½ cup	¾ cup	1 cup
vegetable oil	1 tbs.	1½ tbs.	2 tbs.
honey/maple syrup	1 tbs.	1½ tbs.	2 tbs.
salt	¼ to ½ tsp.	⅓ to ¾ tsp.	½ to 1 tsp.
vital gluten, optional	1 to 2 tbs.	1½ to 3 tbs.	2 to 4 tbs.
multi-grain cereal	⅓ cup	½ cup	⅔ cup
whole wheat flour	1⅔ cups	2½ cups	3⅓ cups
yeast	1 tsp.	1½ tsp.	2 tsp.

flour equivalents: *2 cups*   *3 cups*   *4 cups*
setting: medium   *timer: yes*

Nutritional analysis per 1 oz. slice 80.6 calories, 1.5 g fat (0.2 g sat fat), 3.1 g protein, 14.2 g carbohydrate, 0.1 mg cholesterol, 56.6 mg sodium

12 GRAIN BREAD

This low-rising loaf was developed by request for a 12 grain flour which may be purchased from mail order sources, page 168. Any 7 or 9 grain cereal may also be ground into flour.

	Small	Medium	Large
water/milk	¾ cup	1⅛ cups	1½ cups
fruit concentrate	2 tbs.	3 tbs.	¼ cup
maple syrup/honey	1 tbs.	1½ tbs.	2 tbs.
salt	¼ to ½ tsp.	⅓ to ¾ tsp.	½ to 1 tsp.
vital gluten, optional	1 to 2 tbs.	1½ to 3 tbs.	2 to 4 tbs.
12 grain flour	½ cup	¾ cup	1 cup
whole wheat flour	1½ cups	2¼ cups	3 cups
yeast	1 tsp.	1½ tsp.	2 tsp.
flour equivalents:	*2 cups*	*3 cups*	*4 cup*
setting: medium	*timer: yes with water*		

Nutritional analysis per 1 oz. slice   70.9 calories, 0.5 g fat (0.0 g sat fat), 3.2 g protein, 13.5 g carbohydrate, 0.0 mg cholesterol, 37.8 mg sodium

7 OR 9 GRAIN BREAD   o^k

A wonderful, easy multi-grain bread. Low-rising. Seven or nine grain cereal may be found in most health food stores, and occasionally you may find 4 or 12 also!

	Small	Medium	Large
water/milk	¾ cup	1⅛ cups	1½ cups
fruit juice concentrate	1 tbs.	1½ tbs.	2 tbs.
honey/maple syrup	2 tbs.	3 tbs.	¼ cup
salt	¼ to ½ tsp.	⅓ to ¾ tsp.	½ to 1 tsp.
vital gluten, optional	1 to 2 tbs.	1½ to 3 tbs.	2 to 4 tbs.
7/9 grain cereal	½ cup	¾ cup	1 cup
whole wheat flour	1½ cups	2¼ cups	3 cups
yeast	1 tsp.	1½ tsp.	2 tsp.

flour equivalents: *2 cups*   *3 cups*   *4 cups*
setting: medium   *timer: yes with water*

Nutritional analysis per 1 oz. slice   59.9 calories, 0.4 g fat (0.0 g sat fat), 2.6 g protein, 12.3 g carbohydrate, 0.0 mg cholesterol, 36.9 mg sodium

MULTI-GRAIN BREAD

A hearty, low-rising, densely textured loaf which is sure to please. Serve with a salad and homemade soup for a wonderful, healthy, light meal.

	Small	Medium	Large
water/milk	⅔ cup	1 cup	1⅓ cups
fruit juice concentrate	2 tsp.	1 tbs.	1⅓ tbs.
honey	1 tbs.	1½ tbs.	2 tbs.
salt	¼ to ½ tsp.	⅓ to ¾ tsp.	½ to 1 tsp.
vital gluten, optional	1 to 2 tbs.	1½ to 3 tbs.	2 to 4 tbs.
rye flour	⅓ cup	½ cup	⅔ cup
oats	⅓ cup	½ cup	⅔ cup
whole wheat flour	1⅓ cups	2 cups	2⅔ cups
yeast	1 tsp.	1½ tsp.	2 tsp.
flour equivalents:	*2 cups*	*3 cups*	*4 cups*
setting: medium	*timer: yes with water*		

Nutritional analysis per 1 oz. slice 55.8 calories, 0.4 g fat (0.0 g sat fat), 2.6 g protein, 11.3 g carbohydrate, 0.0 mg cholesterol, 36.8 mg sodium

DIET CORNELL BREAD

This low-rising whole grain bread is based on a formula devised for superior nutrition in bread by faculty at Cornell University. If miso is unavailable, use a fruit juice concentrate and add 1/4 to 1/2 tsp. salt.

	Small	**Medium**	**Large**
water/milk	3/4 cup	1 1/8 cups	1 1/2 cups
miso	1 tbs.	1 1/2 tbs.	2 tbs.
honey	1 tbs.	1 1/2 tbs.	2 tbs.
wheat germ	1 1/2 tbs.	2 1/3 tbs.	3 tbs.
vital gluten, optional	1 to 2 tbs.	1 1/2 to 3 tbs.	2 to 4 tbs.
soy flour	3 tbs.	1/4 cup	1/3 cup
whole wheat flour	2 cups	3 cups	4 cups
nonfat dry milk	3 tbs.	1/4 cup	1/3 cup
yeast	1 1/2 tsp.	2 tsp.	2 1/2 tsp.

flour equivalents: *2 1/3 cups*   *3 1/2 cups*   *4 2/3 cups*
setting: medium   *timer: yes with water*

Nutritional analysis per 1 oz. slice   74.2 calories, 0.6 g fat (0.1 g sat fat), 4.0 g protein, 14.2 g carbohydrate, 0.3 mg cholesterol, 117 mg sodium

ONION RYE

An unbeatable combination. Moisture of onions may vary, so keep an eye on the dough and adjust water or flour if necessary (see page 107).

	Small	**Medium**	**Large**
water	3⁄4 cup	1 1⁄8 cups	1 1⁄2 cups
diced onion	1⁄4 cup	1⁄3 cup	1⁄2 cup
fruit juice concentrate	1 tbs.	1 1⁄2 tbs.	2 tbs.
molasses/honey	1 tbs.	1 1⁄2 tbs.	2 tbs.
salt	1⁄3 tsp.	1⁄2 tsp.	2⁄3 tsp.
caraway seed, optional	1 tsp.	1 1⁄2 tsp.	2 tsp.
vital gluten, optional	1 to 2 tbs.	1 1⁄2 to 3 tbs.	2 to 4 tbs.
rye flour	1⁄2 cup	3⁄4 cup	1 cup
whole wheat flour	2 cups	3 cups	4 cups
yeast	1 1⁄2 tsp.	2 tsp.	2 1⁄2 tsp.

flour equivalents: *2 1⁄2 cups*   *3 3⁄4 cups*   *5 cups*
setting: medium   *timer: yes*

Nutritional analysis per 1 oz. slice   69.2 calories, 0.4 g fat (0.0 g sat fat), 3.1 g protein, 14.3 g carbohydrate, 0.0 mg cholesterol, 50.4 mg sodium

BEAN FLAKE RYE

			Large
			1½ cups
			2
vegetable oil	1 tbs.	1½ tbs.	2 tbs.
molasses	2 tbs.	3 tbs.	¼ cup
salt	¼ tsp.	⅓ tsp.	½ tsp.
black bean flakes	¼ cup	⅓ cup	½ cup
caraway seeds	1 tsp.	1½ tsp.	2 tsp.
orange peel, optional	¼ tsp.	⅓ tsp.	½ tsp.
rye flour	¾ cup	1 cup	1½ cups
vital gluten, optional	1 to 2 tbs.	1½ to 3 tbs.	2 to 4 tbs.
whole wheat flour	1⅔ cups	2½ cups	3⅓ cups
yeast	1 tsp.	1½ tsp.	2 tsp.
flour equivalents:	*2⅔ cups*	*3¾ cups*	*5⅓ cups*
setting: medium	*timer: no (egg)*		

Nutritional analysis per 1 oz. slice 83.9 calories, 1.5 g fat (0.3 g sat fat), 3.6 g protein, 14.9 g carbohydrate, 13.3 mg cholesterol, 55.9 mg sodium

PUMPERNICKEL

This is one of our favorites. Vary the seeds for a real treat. Carob or unsweetened cocoa powders may be substituted for the black bean flakes. Moderate rise.

	Small	Medium	Large
water	1 cup	1½ cups	2 cups
vegetable oil	1 tbs.	1½ tbs.	2 tbs.
molasses	2 tbs.	3 tbs.	4 tbs.
salt	¼ tsp.	⅓ tsp.	½ tsp.
baking soda	1 tsp.	1½ tsp.	2 tsp.
caraway seeds	2 tsp.	1 tbs.	1⅓ tbs.
vital gluten	1 to 2 tbs.	1½ to 2 tbs.	2 to 4 tbs.
black bean flakes	⅓ cup	½ cup	⅔ cup
rye flour	½ cup	¾ cup	1 cup
whole wheat flour	1⅔ cups	2½ cups	3⅓ cups
yeast	1½ tsp.	2 tsp.	2½ tsp.

flour equivalents: *2½ cups*   *3¾ cups*   *5 cups*
setting: medium   *timer: yes*

Nutritional analysis per 1 oz. slice   77 calories, 1.2 g fat (0.2 g sat fat), 3.2 g protein, 14.2 g carbohydrate, 0.0 mg cholesterol, 112 mg sodium

PUMPERNICKEL II

The egg helps to give this a lighter texture. Expect a medium rise.

	Small	**Medium**	**Large**
water/milk	¾ cup	1⅛ cups	1½ cups
egg	1	1½	2
vegetable oil	1 tbs.	1½ tbs.	2 tbs.
molasses	2 tbs.	3 tbs.	¼ cup
salt	¼ tsp.	⅓ tsp.	½ tsp.
black bean flakes	¼ cup	⅓ cup	½ cup
unsweetened cocoa	1 tbs.	1½ tbs.	2 tbs.
caraway seeds	1 tsp.	1½ tsp.	2 tsp.
vital gluten, optional	1 to 2 tbs.	1½ to 3 tbs.	2 to 4 tbs.
rye flour	½ cup	¾ cup	1 cup
whole wheat flour	2 cups	3 cups	4 cups
yeast	1 tsp.	1½ tsp.	2 tsp.

flour equivalents: *2¾ cups*   *4 cups*   *5½ cups*
setting: medium   *timer: no (egg)*

Nutritional analysis per 1 oz. slice   87.9 calories, 1.6 g fat (0.3 g sat fat), 3.8 g protein, 15.7 g carbohydrate, 13.4 mg cholesterol, 58.4 mg sodium

RAISIN PUMPERNICKEL

A terrific variation on a basic pumpernickel. Low- to medium-rising loaf.

	Small	**Medium**	**Large**
buttermilk	1 cup	1½ cups	2 cups
fruit juice concentrate	1 tbs.	1½ tbs.	2 tbs.
molasses	1 tbs.	1½ tbs.	2 tbs.
baking soda	½ tsp.	¾ tsp.	1 tsp.
salt	½ tsp.	¾ tsp.	1 tsp.
vital gluten, optional	1 to 2 tbs.	1½ to 3 tbs.	2 to 4 tbs.
caraway seeds, optional	2 tsp.	1 tbs.	1⅓ tbs.
black bean flakes	1½ tbs.	2⅓ tbs.	3 tbs.
rye flour	½ cup	¾ cup	1 cup
whole wheat flour	2 cups	3 cups	4 cups
yeast	1½ tsp.	2 tsp.	2½ tsp.

raisins	⅓ cup	½ cup	⅔ cup
flour equivalents:	*2½ cups*	*3¾ cups*	*5 cups*
setting: medium	*timer: no-raisin/mix cycle*		

Nutritional analysis per 1 oz. slice 88 calories, 0.5 g fat (0.1 g sat fat), 3.9 g protein, 18.1 g carbohydrate, 0.6 mg cholesterol, 121 mg sodium

RUSSIAN BLACK BREAD

A wonderful black bread. Molasses may be used instead of the barley malt.

	Small	Medium	Large
water	2/3 cup	1 cup	1 1/3 cups
fruit juice concentrate	1 tbs.	1 1/2 tbs.	2 tbs.
barley malt/molasses	1 1/2 tbs.	2 1/3 tbs.	3 tbs.
vinegar	2 tsp.	1 tbs.	1 1/3 tbs.
diced onion	1 tbs.	1 1/2 tbs.	2 tbs.
salt	1/4 tsp.	1/3 tsp.	1/2 tsp.
unsweetened cocoa	1 tbs.	1 1/2 tbs.	2 tbs.
caraway seed	1 tsp.	1 1/2 tsp.	2 tsp.
fennel seed	1/4 tsp.	1/3 tsp.	1/2 tsp.
wheat/oat bran	1/4 cup	1/3 cup	1/2 cup
rye flour	1/2 cup	3/4 cup	1 cup
whole wheat flour	1 3/4 cups	2 2/3 cups	3 1/2 cups
yeast	1 1/2 tsp.	2 tsp.	2 1/2 tsp.
flour equivalents:	*2 1/2 cups*	*3 3/4 cups*	*5 cups*
setting: medium	*timer: yes*		

Nutritional analysis per 1 oz. slice 65.4 calories, 0.4 g fat (0.1 g sat fat), 2.7 g protein, 13.5 g carbohydrate, 0.1 mg cholesterol, 39.5 mg sodium

CORN BREAD

This flavorful corn bread uses corn syrup as the sweetener. Medium rise.

	Small	**Medium**	**Large**
water/milk	¾ cup	1⅛ cups	1½ cups
vegetable oil	1 tbs.	1½ tbs.	2 tbs.
corn syrup	2 tbs.	3 tbs.	4 tbs.
salt	⅓ tsp.	½ tsp.	⅔ tsp.
baking soda	½ tsp.	¾ tsp.	1 tsp.
vital gluten, optional	1 to 2 tbs.	1½ to 3 tbs.	2 to 4 tbs.
cornmeal	½ cup	¾ cup	1 cup
whole wheat flour	2 cups	3 cups	4 cups
yeast	1 tsp.	1½ tsp.	2 tsp.

flour equivalents: *2½ cups*   *3¾ cups*   *5 cups*
setting: medium   *timer: yes with water*

Nutritional analysis per 1 oz. slice   83.6 calories, 1.3 g fat (0.2 g sat fat), 3.1 g protein, 15.9 g carbohydrate, 0.0 mg cholesterol, 88.5 mg sodium

BUTTERMILK CORN BREAD

no "corn" flavor

A lighter corn bread.

	Small	Medium	Large
buttermilk	¾ cup	1⅛ cups	1½ cups
egg	1	1½	2
maple syrup/honey	2 tbs.	3 tbs.	¼ cup
salt	⅓ tsp.	½ tsp.	⅔ tsp.
baking soda	⅓ tsp.	½ tsp.	⅔ tsp.
nutmeg	¼ tsp.	⅓ tsp.	½ tsp.
vital gluten, optional	1 to 2 tbs.	1½ to 3 tbs.	2 to 4 tbs.
cornmeal	½ cup	¾ cup	1 cup
whole wheat flour	2 cups	3 cups	4 cups
yeast	1½ tsp.	2 tsp.	2½ tsp.

flour equivalents: *2½ cups* *3¾ cups* *5 cups*
setting: medium *timer: no (buttermilk, egg)*

Nutritional analysis per 1 oz. slice 84.5 calories, 0.9 g fat (0.2 g sat fat), 3.9 g protein, 16.2 g carbohydrate, 13.7 mg cholesterol, 95.2 mg sodium

ANADAMA BREAD

Anadama is one of those breads which has several different variations. The commonality is that each recipe uses molasses and cornmeal. A hearty bread to serve with soup and salad!

	Small	**Medium**	**Large**
water	⅔ cup	1⅛ cups	1⅓ cups
egg	½	½	1
vegetable oil	1½ tsp.	2 tsp.	1 tbs.
molasses	¼ cup	⅓ cup	½ cup
salt	½ tsp.	⅔ tsp.	¾ tsp.
vital gluten, optional	1 to 2 tbs.	1½ to 3 tbs.	2 to 4 tbs.
cornmeal	¼ cup	⅓ cup	½ cup
whole wheat flour	2 cups	3 cups	4 cups
yeast	1½ tsp.	2 tsp.	2½ tsp.

flour equivalents: *2¼ cups*   *3⅓ cups*   *4½ cups*
setting: medium   *timer: no (egg)*

Nutritional analysis per 1 oz. slice   78.7 calories, 0.9 g fat (0.2 g sat fat), 3.1 g protein, 15.3 g carbohydrate, 6.7 mg cholesterol, 85.5 mg sodium

QUINOA BREAD *pretty good*

Great nutty taste. Quinoa flour is expensive but it is used in small quantities for added nutrition and flavor. Keep the flour refrigerated.

	Small	Medium	Large
water/milk	¾ cup	1⅛ cups	1½ cups
fruit juice concentrate	1 tbs.	1½ tbs.	2 tbs.
honey/maple syrup	1 tbs.	1½ tbs.	2 tbs.
salt	⅓ tsp.	½ tsp.	⅔ tsp.
baking soda	½ tsp.	¾ tsp.	1 tsp.
vital gluten, optional	1 to 2 tbs.	1½ to 3 tbs.	2 to 4 tbs.
sunflower seeds	2 tbs.	3 tbs.	¼ cup
quinoa flour	¼ cup	⅓ cup	½ cup
whole wheat flour	2 cups	3 cups	4 cups
yeast	1½ tsp.	2 tsp.	2½ tsp.

flour equivalents: 2⅓ cups 3½ cups 4¾ cups
setting: medium *timer: yes with water*

Nutritional analysis per 1 oz. slice 79.3 calories, 1.1 g fat (0.1 g sat fat), 3.6 g protein, 14.7 g carbohydrate, 0.0 mg cholesterol, 84.8 mg sodium

CRACKED WHEAT OAT BREAD

The cracked wheat must sit in the liquid for at least one hour (see page 21). A low-rising, nutty tasting loaf.

	Small	**Medium**	**Large**
water	1 cup	1½ cups	2 cups
cracked wheat	⅔ cup	1 cup	1⅓ cups
fruit juice concentrate	1 tbs.	1½ tbs.	2 tbs.
honey/maple syrup	2 tbs.	3 tbs.	4 tbs.
salt	⅓ tsp.	½ tsp.	⅔ tsp.
baking soda	½ tsp.	¾ tsp.	1 tsp.
vital gluten, optional	1 to 2 tbs.	1½ to 3 tbs.	2 to 4 tbs.
oats	½ cup	¾ cup	1 cup
whole wheat flour	1⅔ cups	2½ cups	3⅓ cups
yeast	1 tsp.	1½ tsp.	2 tsp.
flour equivalents:	*2⅔ cups*	*4¼ cups*	*5⅔ cups*
setting: medium	*timer: yes*		

Nutritional analysis per 1 oz. slice   80.7 calories, 0.5 g fat (0.1 g sat fat), 3.4 g protein, 16.8 g carbohydrate, 0.0 mg cholesterol, 75.8 mg sodium

WHOLE WHEAT RAISIN OATMEAL BREAD

A fairly high-rising loaf due to the egg.

	Small	Medium	Large
water/milk	¾ cup	1⅛ cups	1½ cups
egg	1	1½	2
fruit juice concentrate	1 tbs.	1½ tbs.	2 tbs.
maple sugar/sucanet	2 tbs.	3 tbs.	¼ cup
salt	½ tsp.	¾ tsp.	1 tsp.
vital gluten, optional	1 to 2 tbs.	1½ to 3 tbs.	2 to 4 tbs.
oats	½ cup	¾ cup	1 cup
whole wheat flour	2 cups	3 cups	4 cups
yeast	1½ tsp.	2 tsp.	2½ tsp.
raisins	⅓ cup	½ cup	⅔ cup
chopped nuts, optional	¼ cup	⅓ cup	½ cup
flour equivalents:	*2½ cups*	*3¾ cups*	*5 cups*
setting: medium	*timer: no-raisin/mix cycle*		

Nutritional analysis per 1 oz. slice 97.2 calories, 1.9 g fat (0.2 g sat fat), 4.1 g protein, 17.1 g carbohydrate, 13.3 mg cholesterol, 77.4 mg sodium

BUCKWHEAT BREAD

A low-rising bread with lots of buckwheat flavoring.

	Small	Medium	Large
water/milk	¾ cup	1⅛ cups	1½ cups
vegetable oil	1 tbs.	1½ tbs.	2 tbs.
maple syrup/honey	2 tbs.	3 tbs.	4 tbs.
salt	⅓ tsp.	½ tsp.	⅔ tsp.
baking soda	½ tsp.	¾ tsp.	1 tsp.
vital gluten, optional	1 to 2 tbs.	1½ to 3 tbs.	2 to 4 tbs.
buckwheat flour	¼ cup	⅓ cup	½ cup
whole wheat flour	2 cups	3 cups	4 cups
yeast	1½ tsp.	2 tsp.	2½ tsp.

flour equivalents: *2¼ cups*   *3⅓ cups*   *4½ cups*
setting: medium   *timer: yes with water*

Nutritional analysis per 1 oz. slice 73.9 calories, 1.2 g fat (0.2 g sat fat), 2.9 g protein, 13.8 g carbohydrate, 0.0 mg cholesterol, 76.2 mg sodium

KASHA BREAD

Process the raisins and the water in a food processor or blender prior to inserting in the machine. Rises nicely.

	Small	**Medium**	**Large**
water	3⁄4 cup	1 1⁄8 cups	1 1⁄2 cups
raisins	2 tbs.	3 tbs.	1⁄4 cup
egg	1	1 1⁄2	2
fruit juice concentrate	1 tbs.	1 1⁄2 tbs.	2 tbs.
salt	1⁄2 tsp.	3⁄4 tsp.	1 tsp.
vital gluten, optional	1 to 2 tbs.	1 1⁄2 to 3 tbs.	2 to 4 tbs.
buckwheat groats	1⁄4 cup	1⁄3 cup	1⁄2 cup
whole wheat flour	2 cups	3 cups	4 cups
yeast	1 1⁄2 tsp.	2 tsp.	2 1⁄2 tsp.

flour equivalents: 2 1⁄4 cups 3 1⁄3 cups 4 1⁄2 cups
setting: medium *timer: no (egg)*

Nutritional analysis per 1 oz. slice 63.2 calories, 0.6 g fat (0.2 g sat fat), 3.2 g protein, 12 g carbohydrate, 13.3 mg cholesterol, 76.9 mg sodium

PORCUPINE BREAD

A whole grain adaptation of a favorite.

	Small	**Medium**	**Large**
buttermilk	¾ cup	1⅛ cups	1½ cups
fruit juice concentrate	1 tbs.	1½ tbs.	2 tbs.
maple sugar	1 tbs.	1½ tbs.	2 tbs.
salt	¼ to ½ tsp.	⅓ to ¾ tsp.	½ to 1 tsp.
baking soda	¼ tsp.	⅓ tsp.	½ tsp.
vital gluten, optional	1 to 2 tbs.	1½ to 3 tbs.	2 to 4 tbs.
cinnamon	1 tsp.	1½ tsp.	2 tsp.
sesame seeds	1 tbs.	1½ tbs.	2 tbs.
sunflower seeds	2 tbs.	3 tbs.	4 tbs.
raisins	¼ cup	⅓ cup	½ cup
oats	¼ cup	⅓ cup	½ cup
whole wheat flour	2 cups	3 cups	4 cups
yeast	1 tsp.	1½ tsp.	2 tsp.
flour equivalents:	*2⅓ cups*	*3½ cups*	*4¾ cups*
setting: medium	*timer: no-raisin/mix cycle*		

Nutritional analysis per 1 oz. slice   84.6 calories, 1.4 g fat (0.2 g sat fat), 3.8 g protein, 15.3 g carbohydrate, 0.4 mg cholesterol, 72.2 mg sodium

HERB AND CHEESE BREADS

Herbs and spices add zest and flavor to all foods, including bread. Recipes in this section use amounts of dried herb (such as found in the spice section of the grocery store). If fresh herbs are available, consider yourself fortunate and simply triple the amount given in the recipe. The amounts given in the recipe are to my taste; you may prefer stronger or lighter flavoring and should adjust the herbs or spices to your taste.

Use the following chart for ease of converting recipes from dried herbs to fresh:

DRIED	FRESH
1/4 tsp.	3/4 tsp.
1/3 tsp.	1 tsp.
1/2 tsp.	1 1/2 tsp.
2/3 tsp.	2 tsp.
3/4 tsp.	2 1/4 tsp.
1 tsp.	1 tbs.
1 1/2 tsp.	1 1/2 tbs.
2 tsp.	2 tbs.

Fresh herbs and spices really do make a difference and should be used if available. Fresh nutmeg, for example, is easily grated using any kitchen grater.

Whole nutmegs are found in the spice section of your grocery store and only the amount needed should be grated. Many grocery stores sell fresh herbs in the produce section. The less fresh herbs are handled, the better. Rinse briefly and then chop the amount needed. A food processor may be used to chop fresh herbs but they should be processed using the pulse (on/off) button.

Liquid spices which are available in some grocery or gourmet stores may also be used in bread machine baking.

Cheeses also add lots of flavor and nutrition to breads. When measuring cheeses, they should be lightly packed in the cup. Some of the machines may require a slight bit of help getting the dough started as there is a high amount of flour and cheese in some of the recipes. Simply check the dough about 3 to 5 minutes into the initial kneading; if it is not kneading properly take a rubber spatula and gently scrape the sides of the pan, helping the dough towards the kneading paddle.

It is also possible for cheese to affect the moisture of the dough. Flour or water may be adjusted 1 tablespoon at a time until the proper consistency is obtained.

DILL BREAD

Delicious — the amount of dill may be adjusted to taste if desired. Cottage cheese or sour cream may replace the yogurt. If using a granulated sweetener other than fructose, triple the amount.

	Small	Medium	Large
yogurt	⅔ cup	1 cup	1⅓ cups
egg	1	1½	2
fruit juice concentrate	2 tsp.	1 tbs.	1⅓ tbs.
fructose	½ tsp.	¾ tsp.	1 tsp.
dill weed	2 tsp.	1 tbs.	1⅓ tbs.
salt	⅓ tsp.	½ tsp.	⅔ tsp.
baking soda	½ tsp.	¾ tsp.	1 tsp.
vital gluten, optional	1 to 2 tbs.	1½ to 3 tbs.	2 to 4 tbs.
whole wheat flour	2¼ cups	3⅓ cups	4½ cups
yeast	1 tsp.	1½ tsp.	2 tsp.

flour equivalents: *2¼ cups*   *3⅓ cups*   *4½ cups*
setting: medium   *timer: no (yogurt, egg)*

Nutritional analysis per 1 oz. slice   72.7 calories, 0.8 g fat (0.2 g sat fat), 3.9 g protein, 13.3 g carbohydrate, 13.9 mg cholesterol, 85.2 mg sodium

NUTMEG BREAD

This is great — I like freshly grated nutmeg. Cinnamon may be substituted for the nutmeg if desired. A beautiful, high-rising, fluffy loaf.

	Small	**Medium**	**Large**
water	⅔ cup	1 cup	1⅓ cups
egg	1	1½	2
fruit juice concentrate	1 tbs.	1½ tbs.	2 tbs.
honey	2 tbs.	2½ tbs.	3 tbs.
salt	¼ tsp.	¼+ tsp.	⅓ tsp.
nutmeg	⅓ tsp.	⅓+ tsp.	½ tsp.
vital gluten, optional	1 to 2 tbs.	1½ to 3 tbs.	2 to 4 tbs.
whole wheat flour	2¼ cups	3⅓ cups	4½ cups
yeast	1 tsp.	1½ tsp.	2 tsp.

flour equivalents: 2¼ cups   3⅓ cups   4½ cups
setting: medium   timer: no (egg)

Nutritional analysis per 1 oz. slice 74.2 calories, 0.7 g fat (0.1 g sat fat), 3.4 g protein, 14.6 g carbohydrate, 13.3 mg cholesterol, 41 mg sodium

TOMATO BASIL BREAD

Fresh tomato juice makes this bread outstanding. If using commercially canned tomato juice, omit the salt from the recipe. An egg may be mixed in with the juice for a higher rising loaf.

	Small	Medium	Large
tomato juice	7⁄8 cup	1¼ cups	1¾ cups
honey	1 tbs.	1⅓ tbs.	1½ tbs.
basil	1½ tsp.	1¾ tsp.	2 tsp.
salt	½ tsp.	1⅔ tsp.	¾ tsp.
vital gluten, optional	1 to 2 tbs.	1½ to 3 tbs.	2 to 4 tbs.
whole wheat flour	2¼ cups	3⅓ cups	4½ cups
yeast	1½ tsp.	2 tsp.	2½ tsp.

flour equivalents: *2¼ cups*   *3⅓ cups*   *4½ cups*
setting: medium   *timer: yes*

Nutritional analysis per 1 oz. slice   68 calories, 0.3 g fat (0.0 g sat fat), 3.1 g protein, 14.1 g carbohydrate, 0.0 mg cholesterol, 63.4 mg sodium

LEMON POPPY SEED BREAD

not much taste

The combination of lemon and poppy seeds is a sure winner.

	Small	Medium	Large
lemonade	7/8 cup	1 1/4 cups	1 3/4 cups
honey	2 tbs.	2 1/2 tbs.	3 tbs.
salt	1/4 tsp.	1/3 tsp.	1/2 tsp.
lemon peel, optional	1/4 tsp.	1/3 tsp.	1/2 tsp.
poppy seeds	2 tbs.	2 1/2 tbs.	3 tbs.
vital gluten, optional	1 to 2 tbs.	1 1/2 to 3 tbs.	2 to 4 tbs.
whole wheat flour	2 1/2 cups	3 3/4 cups	5 cups
yeast	1 tsp.	1 1/2 tsp.	2 tsp.

flour equivalents: *2 1/4 cups*   *3 1/3 cups*   *4 1/2 cups*
setting: medium   *timer: yes*

Nutritional analysis per 1 oz. slice   82.9 calories, 0.8 g fat (0.1 g sat fat), 3.4 g protein, 16.5 g carbohydrate, 0.0 mg cholesterol, 37.3 mg sodium

SEEDED RYE

A wonderful, flavorful bread due to the combination of seeds. This is great with cream cheese or yogurt cheese.

	Small	**Medium**	**Large**
water	3/4 cup	1 1/8 cups	1 1/2 cups
egg	1	1 1/2	2
fruit juice concentrate	1 1/2 tbs.	2 1/4 tbs.	3 tbs.
honey/maple syrup	1 1/2 tbs.	2 1/4 tbs.	3 tbs.
salt	1/4 tsp.	1/3 tsp.	1/2 tsp.
anise seeds	1/2 tsp.	3/4 tsp.	1 tsp.
fennel seeds	1/2 tsp.	3/4 tsp.	1 tsp.
caraway seeds	1/2 tsp.	3/4 tsp.	1 tsp.
vital gluten, optional	1 to 2 tbs.	1 1/2 to 3 tbs.	2 to 4 tbs.
rye flour	2/3 cup	1 cup	1 1/3 cups
whole wheat flour	2 cups	3 cups	4 cups
yeast	1 1/2 tsp.	2 tsp.	2 1/2 tsp.
flour equivalents:	*2 2/3 cups*	*4 cups*	*5 1/3 cups*
setting: medium	*timer: no (egg)*		

Nutritional analysis per 1 oz. slice 79.2 calories, 0.7 g fat (0.1 g. sat fat), 3.7 g. protein, 15.5 g carbohydrate, 13.3 mg cholesterol, 42.2 mg sodium

CARAWAY RAISIN BREAD

An absolutely outstanding bread with a medium rise. A whole grain twist on Irish soda bread. Use anise or fennel seeds for variation.

	Small	**Medium**	**Large**
milk/water	¾ cup	1⅛ cups	1½ cups
fruit juice concentrate	1 tbs.	1½ tbs.	2 tbs.
honey	2 tbs.	3 tbs.	¼ cup
salt	⅓ tsp.	½ tsp.	⅔ tsp.
caraway seeds	2 tsp.	1 tbs.	1⅓ tbs.
oats	½ cup	¾ cup	1 cup
vital gluten, optional	1 to 2 tbs.	1½ to 3 tbs.	2 to 4 tbs.
whole wheat flour	1½ cups	2¼ cups	3 cups
yeast	1½ tsp.	2 tsp.	2½ tsp.
———			
raisins	⅓ cup	½ cup	⅔ cup
flour equivalents:	*2 cups*	*3 cups*	*4 cups*
setting: medium	*timer: no-raisin/mix cycle*		

Nutritional analysis per 1 oz. slice 65.2 calories, 0.5 g fat (0.1 g sat fat), 3.1 g protein, 13 g carbohydrate, 0.2 mg cholesterol, 42.6 mg sodium

SEEDED BREAD

A crispy crust on a nicely rising, tasty loaf of bread. A winner! Try varying the seeds for different tastes and textures.

	Small	**Medium**	**Large**
water/milk	¾ cup	1⅛ cups	1½ cups
fruit juice concentrate	1 tbs.	1½ tbs.	2 tbs.
honey/maple syrup	1 tbs.	1½ tbs.	2 tbs.
salt	⅓ tsp.	½ tsp.	⅔ tsp.
baking soda	½ tsp.	¾ tsp.	1 tsp.
vital gluten, optional	1 to 2 tbs.	1½ to 3 tbs.	2 to 4 tbs.
sunflower seeds	2 tbs.	3 tbs.	¼ cup
sesame seeds	1 tbs.	1½ tbs.	2 tbs.
flax seeds	1 tbs.	1½ tbs.	2 tbs.
whole wheat flour	2¼ cups	3⅓ cups	4½ cups
yeast	1½ tsp.	2 tsp.	2½ tsp.

flour equivalents: *2½ cups*   *3¾ cups*   *5 cups*
setting: medium   *timer: yes with water*

Nutritional analysis per 1 oz. slice   76 calories, 1 g fat (0.1 g sat fat), 3.7 g protein, 14.1 g carbohydrate, 0.2 mg cholesterol, 85.7 mg sodium

ANCIENT GRAINS BREAD

A delicious bread which is packed with nutrition. Rises nicely.

	Small	**Medium**	**Large**
water/milk	¾ cup	1⅛ cups	1½ cups
fruit juice concentrate	2 tbs.	3 tbs.	4 tbs.
maple/date sugar	1 tbs.	1½ tbs.	2 tbs.
salt	⅓ tsp.	½ tsp.	⅔ tsp.
baking soda	½ tsp.	¾ tsp.	1 tsp.
vital gluten, optional	1 to 2 tbs.	1½ to 3 tbs.	2 to 4 tbs.
quinoa grains	1 tbs.	1½ tbs.	2 tbs.
amaranth grains	1 tbs.	1½ tbs.	2 tbs.
whole wheat flour	2¼ cups	3⅓ cups	4½ cups
yeast	1½ tsp.	2 tsp.	2½ tsp.

flour equivalents: *2⅓ cups*   *3½ cups*   *4⅔ cups*
setting: medium   *timer: yes with water*

Nutritional analysis per 1 oz. slice   72.6 calories, 0.4 g fat (0.1 g sat. fat), 3.6 g protein, 14.4 g carbohydrate, 0.2 mg cholesterol, 80.2 mg sodium

where is the mustard flavor ?

MUSTARD RYE

A very moist bread which rises nicely and has a great taste as well as aroma! We like Dijon or spicy brown mustard. A "must try."

	Small	Medium	Large
water	3/4 cup	1 1/8 cups	1 1/2 cups
egg	1	1 1/2	2
vegetable oil	2 tsp.	1 tbs.	1 1/3 tbs.
honey	1 tbs.	1 1/2 tbs.	2 tbs.
mustard	2 tbs.	3 tbs.	1/4 cup
salt	1/3 tsp.	1/2 tsp.	2/3 tsp.
mustard seeds	1/2 tsp.	3/4 tsp.	1 tsp.
caraway/fennel, optional	1 tsp.	1 1/2 tsp.	2 tsp.
vital gluten, optional	1 to 2 tbs.	1 1/2 to 3 tbs.	2 to 4 tbs.
rye flour	1/2 cup	3/4 cup	1 cup
whole wheat flour	2 cups	3 cups	4 cups
yeast	1 1/2 tsp.	2 tsp.	2 1/2 tsp.
flour equivalents:	*2 1/2 cups*	*3 3/4 cups*	*5 cups*
setting: medium	*timer: no (egg)*		

Nutritional analysis per 1 oz. slice 81.3 calories, 1.3 g fat (0.2 g sat. fat), 3.6 g protein, 14.7 g carbohydrate, 13.3 mg cholesterol, 76.5 mg sodium

OREGANO BREAD

★ ★ definitely tastes like oregano!
makes good sandwich of ham + mustard

Basil or another favorite herb may be substituted for the oregano. This flavorful bread is terrific with lasagna or similar meal. Oregano may be adjusted to taste.

	Small	Medium	Large
water	¾ cup	1⅛ cups	1½ cups
olive oil	1 tbs.	1½ tbs.	2 tbs.
egg	1	1½	2
date/maple sugar	1 tbs.	1⅓ tbs.	1½ tbs.
salt	¼ to ⅓ tsp.	⅓ to ½ tsp.	½ to ⅔ tsp.
oregano	1 tbs.	1½ tbs.	2 tbs.
vital gluten, optional	1 to 2 tbs.	1½ to 3 tbs.	2 to 4 tbs.
whole wheat flour	2¼ cups	3⅓ cups	4½ cups
yeast	1½ tsp.	2 tsp.	2½ tsp.
flour equivalents:	*2¼ cups*	*3⅓ cups*	*4½ cups*
setting: medium	*timer: no (egg)*		

Nutritional analysis per 1 oz. slice 76.6 calories, 1.6 g fat (0.3 g sat fat), 3.4 g protein, 13.2 g carbohydrate, 13.3 mg cholesterol, 41 mg sodium

CARDAMOM SWEET BREAD

Cardamom, common in Scandinavian breads, gives a sweet flavoring.

	Small	Medium	Large
milk/water	¾ cup	1⅛ cups	1½ cups
egg	1	1½	2
fruit juice concentrate	1 tbs.	1½ tbs.	2 tbs.
honey	2 tbs.	3 tbs.	¼ cup
salt	¼ tsp.	⅓ tsp.	½ tsp.
crushed cardamom	½ tsp.	¾ tsp.	1 tsp.
vital gluten, optional	1 to 2 tbs.	1½ to 3 tbs.	2 to 4 tbs.
whole wheat flour	2¼ cups	3⅓ cups	4 cups
yeast	1½ tsp.	2 tsp.	2½ tsp.
———			
raisins, optional	⅓ cup	½ cup	⅔ cup
flour equivalents:	*2¼ cups*	*3⅓ cups*	*4½ cups*
setting: medium	*timer: no-raisin/mix cycle*		

Nutritional analysis per 1 oz. slice 89.6 calories, 0.7 g fat (0.2 g sat fat), 3.9 g protein, 18.2 g carbohydrate, 13.5 mg cholesterol, 47.1 mg sodium

CHEESE HERB BREAD

Use either Swiss or cheddar in this delicious bread. Remember, pack cheese loosely.

	Small	**Medium**	**Large**
water	¾ cup	1⅛ cups	1½ cups
vegetable oil	1 tbs.	1½ tbs.	2 tbs.
fruit juice concentrate	2 tbs.	3 tbs.	¼ cup
grated cheese	⅓ cup	½ cup	⅔ cup
salt	⅓ tsp.	½ tsp.	⅔ tsp.
baking soda	½ tsp.	¾ tsp.	1 tsp.
maple sugar/sucanet	2 tsp.	1 tbs.	1⅓ tbs.
grated Parmesan	2 tbs.	3 tbs.	¼ cup
basil	⅓ tsp.	½ tsp.	⅔ tsp.
parsley	½ tsp.	¾ tsp.	1 tsp.
vital gluten, optional	1 to 2 tbs.	1½ to 3 tbs.	2 to 4 tbs.
whole wheat flour	2¼ cups	3⅓ cups	4½ cups
yeast	1 tsp.	1½ tsp.	2 tsp.

flour equivalents: *2½ cups*   *3¾ cups*   *5 cups*
setting: medium   *timer: no (cheese)*

Nutritional analysis per 1 oz. slice   95.9 calories, 3.1 g fat (1.4 g sat fat), 4.7 g protein, 12.9 g carbohydrate, 5.9 mg cholesterol, 128 mg sodium

PROSCUITTO CHEESE BREAD

The meat and cheese flavor this bread nicely. Proscuitto is a very dry, imported ham. Do not substitute ordinary ham — too much moisture.

	Small	Medium	Large
milk	3⁄4 cup	1 1⁄8 cups	1 1⁄2 cups
fruit concentrate	2 tbs.	3 tbs.	4 tbs.
honey	2 tsp.	1 tbs.	1 1⁄3 tbs.
grated mozzarella	1⁄4 cup	1⁄3 cup	1⁄2 cup
salt	1⁄4 tsp.	1⁄3 tsp.	1⁄2 tsp.
basil (dried)	1⁄2 tsp.	3⁄4 tsp.	1 tsp.
oregano (dried)	1⁄2 tsp.	3⁄4 tsp.	1 tsp.
black pepper (coarse)	1⁄3 tsp.	1⁄2 tsp.	2⁄3 tsp.
vital gluten, optional	1 to 2 tbs.	1 1⁄2 to 3 tbs.	2 to 4 tbs.
whole wheat flour	2 cups	3 cups	4 cups
yeast	1 1⁄2 tsp.	2 tsp.	2 1⁄2 tsp.
diced proscuitto	1⁄4 cup	1⁄3 cup	1⁄2 cup
flour equivalents:	*2 1⁄2 cups*	*3 3⁄4 cups*	*5 cups*
setting: medium	*timer: no-raisin/mix cycle*		

Nutritional analysis per 1 oz. slice 88.9 calories, 2 g fat (0.9 g sat fat), 4.5 g protein, 14 g carbohydrate, 5.6 mg cholesterol, 88 mg sodium

CHEDDAR CHEESE RAISIN BREAD

The testers give this one four stars! Absolutely delicious, a light texture and wonderful flavor! As with most breads in this book, watch moisture.

	Small	**Medium**	**Large**
milk	¾ cup	1⅛ cups	1½ cups
egg	1	1½	2
honey	1 tbs.	1½ tbs.	2 tbs.
grated cheddar	⅔ cup	¾ cup	1 cup
paprika	⅔ tsp.	¾ tsp.	1 tsp.
salt	¼ tsp.	⅓ tsp.	½ tsp.
vital gluten, optional	1 to 2 tbs.	1½ to 3 tbs.	2 to 4 tbs.
whole wheat flour	2¼ cups	3⅓ cups	4½ cups
yeast	1½ tsp.	2 tsp.	2½ tsp.
raisins (dark)	⅓ cup	½ cup	⅔ cup
flour equivalents:	*2¼ cups*	*3⅓ cups*	*4½ cups*
setting: medium	*timer: no-raisin/mix cycle*		

Nutritional analysis per 1 oz. slice 125 calories, 3.8 g fat (2.1 g sat fat), 6.2 g protein, 17.5 g carbohydrate, 23.3 mg cholesterol, 105 mg sodium

CHEESE AND POPPY SEED BREAD

Suggested cheeses are Swiss or cheddar. Be sure to pack the cheese loosely in the cup and scrape the pan if necessary (see page 85).

	Small	**Medium**	**Large**
milk	¾ cup	1⅛ cups	1½ cups
eggs	1	1½	2
fruit juice concentrate	1 tbs.	1½ tbs.	2 tbs.
grated cheese	⅔ cup	¾ cup	1 cup
lemon peel	⅔ tsp.	¾ tsp.	1 tsp.
salt	¼ tsp.	⅓ tsp.	½ tsp.
poppy seeds	1⅓ tbs.	1½ tbs.	2 tbs.
vital gluten, optional	1 to 2 tbs.	1½ to 3 tbs.	2 to 4 tbs.
whole wheat flour	2½ cups	3¾ cups	5 cups
yeast	1½ tsp.	2 tsp.	2½ tsp.

flour equivalents: *2½ cups*   *3¾ cups*   *5 cups*
setting: medium   *timer: no (milk, eggs, cheese)*

Nutritional analysis per 1 oz. slice   107 calories, 3.1 g fat (1.4 g sat fat), 5.9 g protein, 14.6 g carbohydrate, 20.8 mg cholesterol, 81.9 mg sodium

CHEESE BREAD

A flavorful, high-rising bread. Maple sugar or sucanet may be substituted for the fructose but the amount should be tripled.

	Small	**Medium**	**Large**
water/milk	½ cup	¾ cup	1 cup
eggs	2	3	4
fruit juice concentrate	2 tbs.	3 tbs.	¼ cup
grated cheese	½ cup	¾ cup	1 cup
salt	⅓ tsp.	½ tsp.	⅔ tsp.
fructose	¼ tsp.	⅓ tsp.	½ tsp.
baking soda	½ tsp.	¾ tsp.	1 tsp.
vital gluten, optional	1 to 2 tbs.	1½ to 3 tbs.	2 to 4 tbs.
whole wheat flour	2 cups	3 cups	4 cups
yeast	1 tsp.	1½ tsp.	2 tsp.

flour equivalents: *2 cups*   *3 cups*   *4 cups*
setting: medium   *timer: no (eggs, cheese)*

Nutritional analysis per 1 oz. slice   92.9 calories, 3 g fat (1.6 g sat fat), 5.3 g protein, 11.8 g carbohydrate, 20.8 mg cholesterol, 128 mg sodium

CHEDDAR CHEESE AND BACON BREAD

Four stars for this one! Fresh bacon is preferable to bacon bits and should be cooked, drained and crumbled.

	Small	**Medium**	**Large**
milk/water	¾ cup	1⅛ cups	1½ cups
fruit juice concentrate	1 tbs.	1½ tbs.	2 tbs.
grated cheese	½ cup	¾ cup	1 cup
maple/brown sugar	2 tsp.	1 tbs.	1⅓ tbs.
salt	⅓ tsp.	½ tsp.	⅔ tsp.
baking soda	½ tsp.	¾ tsp.	1 tsp.
vital gluten, optional	1 to 2 tbs.	1½ to 3 tbs.	2 to 4 tbs.
whole wheat flour	2¼ cups	3⅓ cups	4½ cups
yeast	1 tsp.	1½ tsp.	2 tsp.
bacon	½ cup	¾ cup	1 cup
flour equivalents:	*2¼ cups*	*3⅓ cups*	*4½ cups*
setting: medium	*timer: no-raisin/mix cycle*		

Nutritional analysis per 1 oz. slice   111 calories, 4 g fat (2 g sat fat), 6 g protein, 13.4 g carbohydrate, 9.7 mg cholesterol, 168 mg sodium

MEXICAN CORN BREAD

The kick comes a few minutes after your first bite.

	Small	Medium	Large
creamed corn	¾ cup	1⅛ cups	1½ cups
fruit juice concentrate	1 tbs.	1½ tbs.	2 tbs.
honey	1 tbs.	1½ tbs.	2 tbs.
grated cheddar	¼ cup	⅓ cup	½ cup
salsa	¼ cup	⅓ cup	½ cup
salt	¼ tsp.	⅓ tsp.	½ tsp.
vital gluten, optional	1 to 2 tbs.	1½ to 3 tbs.	2 to 4 tbs.
cornmeal	½ cup	¾ cup	1 cup
whole wheat flour	2 cups	3 cups	4 cups
yeast	1 tsp.	1½ tsp.	2 tsp.
flour equivalents:	*2½ cups*	*3¾ cups*	*5 cups*
setting: medium	*timer: yes*		

Nutritional analysis per 1 oz. slice 88.6 calories, 1.1 g fat (0.4 g sat fat), 3.7 g protein, 16.9 g carbohydrate, 1.9 mg cholesterol, 132 mg sodium

PEPPERONI BREAD

This low-rising bread is a true winner. A "must try."

	Small	**Medium**	**Large**
water	¾ cup	1⅛ cups	1½ cups
diced pepperoni	⅓ cup	½ cup	⅔ cup
salt	¼ tsp.	⅓ tsp.	½ tsp.
maple sugar/sucanet	1 tsp.	1½ tsp.	2 tsp.
Italian spices	1 tsp.	1½ tsp.	2 tsp.
vital gluten, optional	1 to 2 tbs.	1½ to 3 tbs.	2 to 4 tbs.
whole wheat flour	2¼ cups	3⅓ cups	4½ cups
yeast	1½ tsp.	2 tsp.	2½ tsp.
jalapeño cheese, optional	⅓ cup	½ cup	⅔ cup
diced jalapeño, optional	1	1½	2

flour equivalents: 2¼ cups   3⅓ cups   4½ cups
setting: medium   *timer: no-raisin/mix cycle*

Nutritional analysis per 1 oz. slice   100 calories, 3.6 g fat (1.7 g sat fat), 5 g protein, 12.9 g carbohydrate, 7.6 mg cholesterol, 140 mg sodium

GOLDEN CHEESE BREAD

The combination of cheeses and seeds is wonderful. High-rising loaf.

	Small	Medium	Large
buttermilk	7/8 cup	1¼ cups	1¾ cups
fruit juice concentrate	1 tbs.	1½ tbs.	2 tbs.
egg	1	1½	2
grated cheddar	¼ cup	⅓ cup	½ cup
crumbled blue cheese	2 tbs.	3 tbs.	¼ cup
salt	¼ tsp.	⅓ tsp.	½ tsp.
coarse black pepper	¼ tsp.	⅓ tsp.	½ tsp.
caraway seeds	1 tsp.	1½ tsp.	2 tsp.
vital gluten, optional	1 to 2 tbs.	1½ to 3 tbs.	2 to 4 tbs.
wheat/oat flakes	½ cup	¾ cup	1 cup
whole wheat flour	2 cups	3 cups	4 cups
yeast	1 tsp.	1½ tsp.	2 tsp.

flour equivalents: 2½ cups   3¾ cups   5 cups
setting: medium   timer: no (buttermilk, egg, cheese)

Nutritional analysis per 1 oz. slice   180 calories, 2 g fat (0.7 g sat fat), 8.2 g protein, 32.9 g carbohydrate, 16.2 mg cholesterol, 75.7 mg sodium

FRUIT AND VEGETABLE BREADS

Many of the recipes in this section use the fruit themselves as a source of liquid for the bread. As the moisture content of individual fruits or vegetables may vary, it is important to check the dough after the first 3 to 5 minutes of kneading. If the dough appears dry, crumbly or forms two or more balls, add water or milk one tablespoon at a time until one smooth ball of dough is obtained. If the dough appears too wet and is unable to form a ball of dough, add one tablespoon of flour at a time until it does. In addition, recipes which use fruits as part of the liquid for the recipe may have difficulty blending the ingredients during the initial kneading. If necessary, scrape the sides of the pans to loosen the ingredients and to help get them moving by the kneading paddle. Recipes are given with amounts which have worked during testing, but these variables exist.

APPLE BREAD

Try this terrific, low-rising bread toasted with hot apple butter for a real treat! I like to use Brazil nuts.

	Small	Medium	Large
apple juice	2/3 cup	1 cup	1 1/3 cups
applesauce	2 tbs.	3 tbs.	1/4 cup
honey	2 tbs.	3 tbs.	1/4 cup
salt	1/4 tsp.	1/3 tsp.	1/2 tsp.
cinnamon	1/4 tsp.	1/3 tsp.	1/2 tsp.
vital gluten, optional	1 to 2 tbs.	1 1/2 to 3 tbs.	2 to 4 tbs.
whole wheat flour	2 cups	3 cups	4 cups
yeast	1 tsp.	1 1/2 tsp.	2 tsp.
————			
chopped nuts, optional	1/3 cup	1/2 cup	2/3 cup

flour equivalents: *2 cups* *3 cups* *4 cups*
setting: light to medium *timer: no-raisin/mix cycle*

Nutritional analysis per 1 oz. slice 68.6 calories, 0.7 g fat (0.1 g sat fat), 2.6 g protein, 14.1 g carbohydrate, 0.0 mg cholesterol, 36.9 mg sodium

APPLE AMARANTH BREAD

What a sweet, flavorful whole grain bread — almost like a coffee cake. Great with coffee in the morning or with peanut butter for a nutritious snack. Apple juice concentrate may be used in place of the applesauce if desired.

	Small	**Medium**	**Large**
apple juice	⅔ cup	1 cup	1⅓ cups
applesauce	2 tbs.	3 tbs.	¼ cup
honey	2 tbs.	3 tbs.	¼ cup
almond extract	2 tsp.	1 tbs.	1⅓ tbs.
salt	¼ tsp.	⅓ tsp.	½ tsp.
vital gluten, optional	1 to 2 tbs.	1½ to 3 tbs.	2 to 4 tbs.
amaranth flour	½ cup	¾ cup	1 cup
whole wheat flour	1½ cups	2¼ cups	3 cups
yeast	1 tsp.	1½ tsp.	2 tsp.
chopped almonds	¼ cup	⅓ cup	½ cup
flour equivalents:	*2 cups*	*3 cups*	*4 cups*
setting: light	*timer: no-raisin/mix cycle*		

Nutritional analysis per 1 oz. slice   94.2 calories, 1.8 g fat (0.1 g sat fat), 3.6 g protein, 16.9 g carbohydrate, 0.0 mg cholesterol, 50.2 mg sodium

ORANGE BREAD

A wonderful bread with a tangy, light orange taste — great moist texture. Rises nicely.

	Small	Medium	Large
milk/water	⅔ cup	1 cup	1⅓ cups
orange juice concentrate	⅓ cup	½ cup	⅔ cup
honey	1½ tbs.	2⅓ tbs.	3 tbs.
vital gluten, optional	1 to 2 tbs.	1½ to 3 tbs.	2 to 4 tbs.
~~grated orange peel, optional~~ *orange oil*	½ tsp.	¾ tsp.	1 tsp.
whole wheat flour	2 cups	3 cups	4 cups
yeast	1½ tsp.	2 tsp.	2½ tsp.

flour equivalents: *2 cups*   *3 cups*   *4 cups*
setting: light to medium   *timer: yes with water*

Nutritional analysis per 1 oz. slice   65.6 calories, 0.3 g fat (0.0 g sat fat), 3.1 g protein, 13.2 g carbohydrate, 0.2 mg cholesterol, 6.0 mg sodium

APPLE OAT BREAD

A fairly low-rising delicious bread. The pumpkin pie spice (which may be adjusted to taste) really gives it the extra flavor.

	Small	**Medium**	**Large**
apple juice	3/4 cup	1 1/8 cups	1 1/2 cups
applesauce	1 tbs.	1 1/2 tbs.	2 tbs.
apple juice concentrate	1 tbs.	1 1/2 tbs.	2 tbs.
honey	1 tbs.	1 1/2 tbs.	2 tbs.
salt	1/4 tsp.	1/3 tsp.	1/2 tsp.
pumpkin pie spice	1/2 tsp.	3/4 tsp.	1 tsp.
vital gluten, optional	1 to 2 tbs.	1 1/2 to 3 tbs.	2 to 4 tbs.
wheat/oat flakes	1/2 cup	3/4 cup	1 cup
whole wheat flour	1 1/2 cups	2 1/4 cups	3 cups
yeast	1 tsp.	1 1/2 tsp.	2 tsp.

flour equivalents: *2 cups*   *3 cups*   *4 cups*
setting: medium   *timer: yes*

Nutritional analysis per 1 oz. slice   100 calories, 0.5 g fat (0.1 g sat fat), 2.7 g protein, 22.2 g carbohydrate, 0.0 mg cholesterol, 39.3 mg sodium

ZUCCHINI BREAD

A high-rising whole grain bread with a very slight flavor of zucchini — a great use for garden extras! Fruit juice concentrate may replace the oil.

	Small	Medium	Large
zucchini, grated	1/3 cup	1/2 cup	2/3 cup
water	1/2 cup	3/4 cup	1 cup
walnut oil	2 tbs.	3 tbs.	1/4 cup
honey	2 tbs.	3 tbs.	1/4 cup
salt	1/4 tsp.	1/3 tsp.	1/2 tsp.
cinnamon	1/3 to 1/2 tsp.	1/2 to 3/4 tsp.	2/3 to 1 tsp.
vital gluten, optional	1 to 2 tbs.	1 1/2 to 3 tbs.	2 to 4 tbs.
whole wheat flour	1 1/2 cups	2 1/4 cups	3 cups
oat flour	1/2 cup	3/4 cup	1 cup
yeast	1 1/2 tsp.	2 tsp.	2 1/2 tsp.
———			
walnuts, chopped	1/4 cup	1/3 cup	1/2 cup
flour equivalents:	*2 cups*	*3 cups*	*4 cups*
setting: medium	*timer: no-raisin/mix cycle*		

Nutritional analysis per 1 oz. slice 104 calories, 3.2 g fat (0.5 g sat fat), 3.6 g protein, 16.3 g carbohydrate, 0.0 mg cholesterol, 37.1 mg sodium

FIG BREAD

A twist on a date bread. This medium-rising loaf is great with chunky chicken or tuna salad. Easy to slice.

	Small	**Medium**	**Large**
milk/water	¾ cup	1⅛ cups	1½ cups
walnut oil/butter	1 tbs.	1½ tbs	2 tbs.
maple sugar/sucanet	1 tbs.	1½ tbs.	2 tbs.
salt	¼ tsp.	⅓ tsp.	½ tsp.
vital gluten, optional	1 to 2 tbs.	1½ to 3 tbs.	2 to 4 tbs.
whole wheat flour	2 cups	3 cups	4 cups
yeast	1 tsp.	1½ tsp.	2 tsp.
chopped figs	⅓ cup	½ cup	⅔ cup
chopped walnuts	¼ cup	⅓ cup	½ cup
flour equivalents:	*2 cups*	*3 cups*	*4 cups*
setting: medium	*timer: no-raisin/mix cycle*		

Nutritional analysis per 1 oz. slice   89.8 calories, 2.3 g fat (0.3 g sat fat), 3.7 g protein, 14.7 g carbohydrate, 0.2 mg cholesterol, 42.9 mg sodium

APPLE OAT MILLET BREAD

A flavorful bread which is sure to be a true hit! The cinnamon may be adjusted to taste if desired. Rises moderately high.

	Small	Medium	Large
apple juice	¾ cup	1⅛ cups	1½ cups
honey	2 tbs.	3 tbs.	¼ cup
applesauce	2 tbs.	3 tbs.	¼ cup
salt	¼ tsp.	⅓ tsp.	½ tsp.
cinnamon	¼ tsp.	⅓ tsp.	½ tsp.
vital gluten, optional	1 to 2 tbs.	1½ to 3 tbs.	2 to 4 tbs.
millet flour	⅓ cup	½ cup	⅔ cup
oat flakes	⅓ cup	½ cup	⅔ cup
whole wheat flour	1⅓ cups	2 cups	2⅔ cups
yeast	1½ tsp.	2 tsp.	2½ tsp.
raisins	¼ cup	⅓ cup	½ cup
chopped nuts, optional	2 to 3 tbs.	3 to 4 tbs.	4 to 5 tbs.
flour equivalents:	*2 cups*	*3 cups*	*4 cups*
setting: medium	*timer: no-raisin/mix cycle*		

Nutritional analysis per 1 oz. slice 87.3 calories, 1.1 g fat (0.1 g sat fat), 3.2 g protein, 17.7 g carbohydrate, 0.0 mg cholesterol, 37.4 mg sodium

BANANA BREAD ✳ ⊀

A nice, sweet banana flavor. The oil may be omitted and replaced with extra buttermilk. Watch the dough as the banana may affect the moisture (see page 107).

	Small	Medium	Large
buttermilk	½ cup	¾ cup	1 cup
mashed banana	¼ cup	⅓ cup	½ cup
eggs	1	1½	2
vegetable oil	1 tbs.	1½ tbs.	2 tbs.
honey	2 tbs.	3 tbs.	¼ cup
salt	¼ tsp.	⅓ tsp.	½ tsp.
cinnamon	¼ tsp.	⅓ tsp.	½ tsp.
baking soda	¼ tsp.	⅓ tsp.	½ tsp.
vital gluten, optional	1 to 2 tbs.	1½ to 3 tbs.	2 to 4 tbs.
whole wheat flour	1½ cups	2¼ cups	3 cups
oats	½ cup	¾ cup	1 cup
yeast	1 tsp.	1½ tsp.	2 tsp.
flour equivalents:	*2 cups*	*3 cups*	*4 cups*
setting: medium	*timer: no (buttermilk, eggs)*		

Nutritional analysis per 1 oz. slice 78.8 calories, 1.6 g fat (0.1 g sat fat), 3.4 g protein, 13.5 g carbohydrate, 13.6 mg cholesterol, 61.5 mg sodium

APPLE CHUNK BREAD

The diced and peeled apples do lend some additional moisture to the dough and may be added at the beginning or at the beep. Watch the dough and add water or flour if necessary and scrape the sides of the pan if it is not mixing properly.

	Small	Medium	Large
apple juice	¾ cup	1⅛ cups	1½ cups
honey	2 tbs.	3 tbs.	¼ cup
salt	⅓ tsp.	½ tsp.	⅔ tsp.
baking soda	½ tsp.	¾ tsp.	1 tsp.
cinnamon	⅓ tsp.	½ tsp.	⅔ tsp.
vital gluten, optional	1 to 2 tbs.	1½ to 3 tbs.	2 to 4 tbs.
oats	½ cup	¾ cup	1 cup
whole wheat flour	2¼ cups	3⅓ cups	4½ cups
yeast	1 tsp.	1½ tsp.	2 tsp.
diced, peeled apple	½	¾	1
flour equivalents:	*2¾ cups*	*4+ cups*	*5½ cups*
setting: medium	*timer: no-raisin/mix cycle*		

Nutritional analysis per 1 oz. slice 86.4 calories, 0.5 g fat (0.1 g sat fat), 3.4 g protein, 18.1 g carbohydrate, 0.0 mg cholesterol, 74.8 mg sodium

CARROT BREAD

A wonderful carrot bread. Not sweet like a baking powder-leavened carrot bread but nice taste and texture.

	Small	Medium	Large
water/milk	2/3 cup	1 cup	1 1/3 cups
grated carrot	1/2 cup	3/4 cup	1 cup
maple sugar/sucanet	1 tbs.	1 1/2 tbs.	2 tbs.
cinnamon	1/4 tsp.	1/3 tsp.	1/2 tsp.
salt	1/3 tsp.	1/2 tsp.	2/3 tsp.
vital gluten, optional	1 to 2 tbs.	1 1/2 to 3 tbs.	2 to 4 tbs.
wheat/oat flakes	3/4 cup	1 1/8 cups	1 1/2 cups
whole wheat flour	1 1/2 cups	2 1/4 cups	3 cups
yeast	1 tsp.	1 1/2 tsp.	2 tsp.

flour equivalents: *2 1/4 cups*   *3 1/3 cups*   *4 1/2 cups*
setting: medium   *timer: yes with water*

Nutritional analysis per 1 oz. slice   85.6 calories, 0.4 g fat (0.0 g sat fat), 3.8 g protein, 17.2 g carbohydrate, 0.0 mg cholesterol, 50.3 mg sodium

STOLLEN

A whole grain, natural sugar variation on a favorite holiday bread. Regular dried fruit may also be used. Heavy amounts of added fruit may cause the bread not to cook properly, so be careful if you increase the amount given.

	Small	Medium	Large
milk/water	½ cup	¾ cup	1 cup
fruit juice concentrate	⅓ cup	½ cup	⅔ cup
egg	1	1½	2
almond extract	¼ tsp.	⅓ tsp.	½ tsp.
fructose	1 tbs.	1½ tbs.	2 tbs.
salt	⅓ tsp.	½ tsp.	⅔ tsp.
baking soda	½ tsp.	¾ tsp.	1 tsp.
mace	⅛ tsp.	⅛+ tsp.	¼ tsp.
cardamom	⅛ tsp.	⅛+ tsp.	¼ tsp.
grated lemon peel	1 tsp.	1½ tsp.	2 tsp.
vital gluten, optional	1 to 2 tbs.	1½ to 3 tbs.	2 to 4 tbs.
whole wheat flour	2¼ cups	3⅓ cups	4½ cups
yeast	1 tsp.	1½ tsp.	2 tsp.

| mixed candied fruit | ¼ cup | ⅓ cup | ½ cup |
| chopped almonds | 2 tbs. | 3 tbs. | ¼ cup |

| *flour equivalents:* | 2¼ cups | 3⅓ cups | 4½ cups |
| *setting: medium* | *timer: no-raisin/mix cycle* | | |

Nutritional analysis per 1 oz. slice 76.3 calories, 1.2 g fat (0.2 g sat fat), 3.8 g protein, 13.5 g carbohydrate, 13.4 mg cholesterol, 88.6 mg sodium

ORANGE MULTI-GRAIN BREAD

Raisins or dried cranberries can be added to this tasty, medium-rising loaf.

	Small	Medium	Large
orange juice	7/8 cup	1¼ cups	1¾ cups
egg	1	1½	2
honey	1 tbs.	1½ tbs.	2 tbs.
salt	½ tsp.	¾ tsp.	1 tsp.
vital gluten, optional	1 to 2 tbs.	1½ to 3 tbs.	2 to 4 tbs.
7 or 9 grain cereal	½ cup	¾ cup	1 cup
wheat flour	2 cups	3 cups	4 cups
yeast	1½ tsp.	2 tsp.	2½ tsp.

flour equivalents:	*2¼ cups*	*3⅓ cups*	*4½ cups*
setting: medium	*timer: no (egg)*		

Nutritional analysis per 1 oz. slice   94.7 calories, 0.9 g fat (0.1 g sat fat), 4.2 g protein, 17.9 g carbohydrate, 13.3 mg cholesterol, 76.9 mg sodium

APPLE OATMEAL BREAD

ok flavor

This is great! Serve toasted with apple butter in the fall.

	Small	Medium	Large
apple juice	¾ cup	1⅛ cups	1½ cups
egg	1	1½	2
honey	2 tbs.	3 tbs.	¼ cup
salt	⅓ tsp.	½ tsp.	⅔ tsp.
cinnamon	¼ tsp.	⅓ tsp.	½ tsp.
vital gluten, optional	1 to 2 tbs.	1½ to 3 tbs.	2 to 4 tbs.
oat flakes	½ cup	¾ cup	1 cup
whole wheat flour	2 cups	3 cups	4 cups
yeast	1½ tsp.	2 tsp.	2½ tsp.
diced dried apples	⅓ cup	½ cup	⅔ cup
chopped nuts, optional	¼ cup	⅓ cup	½ cup

flour equivalents: 2½ cups   3¾ cups   5 cups
setting: medium   *timer: no-raisin/mix cycle*

Nutritional analysis per 1 oz. slice 117 calories, 1.9 g fat (0.2 g sat fat), 3.8 g protein, 20.8 g carbohydrate, 13.3 mg cholesterol, 58.9 mg sodium

APPLE RAISIN BREAD

A combination of two favorite breads — wonderful. Fresh, peeled, diced apples may replace the dried apples but the apple juice should be decreased slightly.

	Small	Medium	Large
apple juice	¾ cup	1⅛ cups	1½ cups
egg	1	1½	2
maple sugar/sucanet	1½ tbs.	2⅓ tbs.	3 tbs.
salt	⅓ tsp.	½ tsp.	⅔ tsp.
cinnamon	¼ tsp.	⅓ tsp.	½ tsp.
vital gluten, optional	1 to 2 tbs.	1½ to 3 tbs.	2 to 4 tbs.
whole wheat flour	2½ cups	3¾ cups	5 cups
yeast	1½ tsp.	2 tsp.	2½ tsp.
diced dried apples	¼ cup	⅓ cup	½ cup
raisins	¼ cup	⅓ cup	½ cup
flour equivalents:	*2½ cups*	*3¾ cups*	*5 cups*
setting: medium	*timer: no-raisin/mix cycle*		

Nutritional analysis per 1 oz. slice 98.7 calories, 0.7 g fat (0.1 g sat fat), 3.8 g protein, 20.8 g carbohydrate, 13.3 mg cholesterol, 56.1 mg sodium

APPLE CARROT BREAD

A low-rising bread, but really delicious.

	Small	Medium	Large
apple juice	¾ cup	1⅛ cups	1½ cups
grated carrots	¼ cup	⅓ cup	½ cup
egg	1	1½	2
maple syrup/honey	1½ tbs.	2⅓ tbs.	3 tbs.
salt	⅓ tsp.	½ tsp.	⅔ tsp.
cinnamon	¼ tsp.	⅓ tsp.	½ tsp.
vital gluten, optional	1 to 2 tbs.	1½ to 3 tbs.	2 to 4 tbs.
wheat/oat flakes	½ cup	¾ cup	1 cup
whole wheat flour	2 cups	3 cups	4 cups
yeast	1½ tsp.	2 tsp.	2½ tsp.
———			
diced dried apples	¼ cup	⅓ cup	½ cup
chopped nuts, optional	¼ cup	⅓ cup	½ cup

flour equivalents: *2½ cups*   *3¾ cups*   *5 cups*
setting: medium   *timer: no-raisin/mix cycle*

Nutritional analysis per 1 oz. slice   118 calories, 1.9 g fat (0.2 g sat fat), 4.7 g protein, 22 g carbohydrate, 13.3 mg cholesterol, 57.4 mg sodium

COCONUT CHERRY BREAD

This is a wonderful tasting, high-rising and colorful loaf.

	Small	Medium	Large
milk/water	¾ cup	1⅛ cups	1½ cups
honey	1 tbs.	1½ tbs.	2 tbs.
grated carrots	¼ cup	⅓ cup	½ cup
chopped maraschino cherries	12	18	24
salt	⅓ tsp.	½ tsp.	⅔ tsp.
coconut flakes	⅓ cup	½ cup	⅔ cup
cinnamon	⅓ tsp.	½ tsp.	⅔ tsp.
vital gluten, optional	1 to 2 tbs.	1½ to 3 tbs.	2 to 4 tbs.
wheat/oat flakes	¼ cup	⅓ cup	½ cup
whole wheat flour	2 cups	3 cup	4 cups
yeast	1½ tsp.	2 tsp.	2½ tsp.

flour equivalents: *2¼ cups*   *3⅓ cups*   *4½ cups*
setting: medium   *timer: yes*

Nutritional analysis per 1 oz. slice   91.4 calories, 1.3 g fat (0.8 g sat fat), 3.8 g protein, 17.2 g carbohydrate, 0.2 mg cholesterol, 61.6 mg sodium

BERRY BREAD

A light, airy, high-rising bread with just a hint of berry flavor. See page 21 for directions on pureeing fruit.

	Small	Medium	Large
buttermilk	½ cup	¾ cup	1 cup
berry puree	¼ cup	⅓ cup	½ cup
egg	1	1½	2
honey	1 tbs.	1½ tbs.	2 tbs.
baking soda	¼ tsp.	⅓ tsp.	½ tsp.
salt	¼ tsp.	⅓ tsp.	½ tsp.
vital gluten, optional	1 to 2 tbs.	1½ to 3 tbs.	2 to 4 tbs.
whole wheat flour	2¼ cups	3⅓ cups	4½ cups
yeast	1 tsp.	1½ tsp.	2 tsp.

flour equivalents: *2¼ cups*   *3⅓ cups*   *4½ cups*
setting: medium   *timer: no (buttermilk, egg)*

Nutritional analysis per 1 oz. slice   73.6 calories, 0.7 g fat (0.2 g sat fat), 3.6 g protein, 14 g carbohydrate, 13.6 mg cholesterol, 61.5 mg sodium

CHOCOLATE COCONUT BREAD

Four stars! This bread rises nicely.

	Small	**Medium**	**Large**
heavy cream/milk	2/3 cup	1 cup	1 1/3 cups
egg	1	1 1/2	2
fruit juice concentrate	2 tbs.	3 tbs.	4 tbs.
honey/maple syrup	2 tbs.	3 tbs.	1/4 cup
unsweetened cocoa	1 tbs.	1 1/2 tbs.	2 tbs.
salt	1/4 tsp.	1/3 tsp.	1/2 tsp.
coconut flakes	1/4 cup	1/3 cup	1/2 cup
vital gluten, optional	1 to 2 tbs.	1 1/2 to 3 tbs.	2 to 4 tbs.
wheat/oat flakes	1/2 cup	3/4 cup	1 cup
whole wheat flour	2 cups	3 cups	4 cups
yeast	1 tsp.	1 1/2 tsp.	2 tsp.
chocolate chips	1/3 cup	1/2 cup	2/3 cup
chopped nuts	1/4 cup	1/3 cup	1/2 cup
flour equivalents:	*2 1/2 cups*	*3 3/4 cups*	*5 cups*

setting: medium   *timer: no-raisin/mix cycle*

Nutritional analysis per 1 oz. slice   139 calories, 6.4 g fat (3.2 g sat fat), 4.4 g protein, 17.4 g carbohydrate, 27 mg cholesterol, 51.6 mg sodium

LEMON BREAD

A light and airy bread with a hint of lemon. Serve toasted with a lemon topping for a delectable treat. Yogurt or buttermilk may be used instead of the sour cream.

	Small	**Medium**	**Large**
sour cream	1/4 cup	1/3 cup	1/2 cup
milk	1/3 cup	1/2 cup	2/3 cup
fruit juice concentrate	1 1/2 tbs.	2 1/3 tbs.	3 tbs.
eggs	1	1 1/2	2
honey	1 1/2 tbs.	2 tbs.	3 tbs.
baking soda	1/4 tsp.	1/3 tsp.	1/2 tsp.
grated lemon peel	1/4 tsp.	1/3 tsp.	1/2 tsp.
salt	1/4 tsp.	1/3 tsp.	1/2 tsp.
vital gluten, optional	1 to 2 tbs.	1 1/2 to 3 tbs.	2 to 4 tbs.
whole wheat flour	2 1/4 cups	3 1/3 cups	4 1/2 cups
yeast	1 1/2 tsp.	2 tsp.	2 1/2 tsp.

flour equivalents: *2 1/4 cups*   *3 1/3 cups*   *4 1/2 cups*
setting: medium   *timer: no (sour cream, milk, egg)*

Nutritional analysis per 1 oz. slice   81.7 calories, 1.4 g fat (0.6 g sat fat), 3.7 g protein, 14.5 g carbohydrate, 15 mg cholesterol, 58.1 mg sodium

COCONUT BREAD

This is an outstanding bread — great with breakfast or as a snack. For variation add white chocolate chips and/or nuts; 1/4, 1/3 or 1/2 cup.

	Small	Medium	Large
milk/water	3/4 cup	1 1/8 cups	1 1/2 cups
coconut extract	2 tsp.	1 tbs.	1 1/3 tbs.
fruit juice concentrate	1 tbs.	1 1/4 tbs.	1 1/2 tbs.
egg	1	1 1/2	2
honey	2 tbs.	3 tbs.	4 tbs.
salt	1/4 tsp.	1/3 tsp.	1/2 tsp.
coconut flakes	1/4 cup	1/3 cup	1/2 cup
vital gluten, optional	1 to 2 tbs.	1 1/2 to 3 tbs.	2 to 4 tbs.
whole wheat flour	2 1/4 cups	3 1/3 cups	4 1/2 cups
yeast	1 1/2 tsp.	2 tsp.	2 1/2 tsp.

flour equivalents: *2 1/4 cups*   *3 1/3 cups*   *4 1/2 cups*
setting: medium   *timer: no (milk, egg)*

Nutritional analysis per 1 oz. slice   86.5 calories, 1.2 g fat (0.6 g sat fat), 3.8 g protein, 16 g carbohydrate, 13.5 mg cholesterol, 50.5 mg sodium

PUMPKIN APPLE BREAD

Delicious. Diced dried apple and nuts are optional. Fresh cooked pureed pumpkin is preferred but canned pumpkin does nicely also.

	Small	Medium	Large
pumpkin	¼ cup	⅓ cup	½ cup
apple juice	½ cup	¾ cup	1 cup
egg	1	1½	2
honey	2 tbs.	3 tbs.	¼ cup
pumpkin pie spice	1 tsp.	1½ tsp.	2 tsp.
salt	⅓ tsp.	¼ tsp.	⅔ tsp.
vital gluten, optional	1 to 2 tbs.	1½ to 3 tbs.	2 to 4 tbs.
oats/wheat flakes	½ cup	¾ cup	1 cup
whole wheat flour	2 cups	3 cups	4 cups
yeast	1½ tsp.	2 tsp.	2½ tsp.
dried apple, diced	¼ cup	⅓ cup	½ cup
ground nuts	2 tbs.	3 tbs.	¼ cup
flour equivalents:	*2½ cups*	*3¾ cups*	*5 cups*
setting: medium	*timer: no-raisin/mix cycle*		

Nutritional analysis per 1 oz. slice   97.5 calories, 1.3 g fat (0.2 g sat fat), 3.9 g protein, 18.9 g carbohydrate, 13.3 mg cholesterol, 55.6 mg sodium

WHOLE ORANGE BREAD

A wonderful, very tasty bread. As the oranges provide the moisture and moisture content of individual fruits vary, watch the dough and add water a tablespoon at a time if necessary until the dough forms a round ball. See page 107.

	Small	Medium	Large
water	1 tbs. at time if necessary		
mandarin orange segments	1 cup	1½ cup	2 cups
orange juice concentrate	1 tbs.	1½ tbs.	2 tbs.
egg	1	1½	2
maple sugar/sucanet	1 tbs.	1½ tbs.	2 tbs.
salt	⅓ tsp.	½ tsp.	⅔ tsp.
vital gluten, optional	1 to 2 tbs.	1½ to 3 tbs.	2 to 4 tbs.
whole wheat flour	2¼ cups	3⅓ cups	4½ cups
yeast	1½ tsp.	2 tsp.	2½ tsp.
flour equivalents:	*2¼ cups*	*3⅓ cups*	*4½ cups*
setting: medium	*timer: no (egg)*		

Nutritional analysis per 1 oz. slice 78.1 calories, 0.7 g fat (0.1 g sat fat), 3.6 g protein, 15.5 g carbohydrate, 13.3 mg cholesterol, 52.6 mg sodium

ORANGE APRICOT BREAD

This combination is sure to please the apricot lover in your family. A true winner! Thanks to Brian Bird for requesting this one.

	Small	Medium	Large
orange juice	¾ cup	1⅛ cups	1½ cups
egg	1	1½	2
honey	1 tbs.	1½ tbs.	2 tbs.
salt	½ tsp.	¾ tsp.	1 tsp.
orange peel, optional	¼ tsp.	⅓ tsp.	½ tsp.
vital gluten, optional	1 to 2 tbs.	1½ to 3 tbs.	2 to 4 tbs.
whole wheat flour	2¼ cups	3⅓ cups	4½ cups
yeast	1 tsp.	1½ tsp.	2 tsp.
─────			
diced dried apricots	¼ cup	⅓ cup	½ cup

flour equivalents:	*2¼ cups*	*3⅓ cups*	*4½ cups*
setting: medium	*timer: no- raisin/mix cycle*		

Nutritional analysis per 1 oz. slice 80.2 calories, 0.7 g fat (0.1 g sat fat), 3.5 g protein, 16.1 g carbohydrate, 13.3 mg cholesterol, 76.8 mg sodium

BANANA AMARANTH BREAD

Amaranth is a great source of protein and combines nicely with banana in this loaf. Be sure to watch the dough for adequate moisture.

	Small	**Medium**	**Large**
milk	½ cup	¾ cup	1 cup
mashed banana	¼ cup	⅓ cup	½ cup
egg	1	1½	2
honey	2 tbs.	3 tbs.	¼ cup
salt	¼ tsp.	⅓+ tsp.	½ tsp.
cinnamon	⅛ tsp.	⅛+ tsp.	¼ tsp.
vital gluten, optional	1 to 2 tbs.	1½ to 3 tbs.	2 to 4 tbs.
amaranth flour	¼ cup	⅓ cup	½ cup
whole wheat flour	2¼ cups	3⅓ cups	4½ cups
yeast	1½ tsp.	2 tsp.	2½ tsp.
chopped nuts, optional	¼ cup	⅓ cup	½ cup
flour equivalents:	*2½ cups*	*3¾ cups*	*5 cups*
setting: light to medium	*timer: no-raisin/mix*		

Nutritional analysis per 1 oz. slice   104 calories, 2 g fat (0.2 g sat fat), 4.7 g protein, 18.2 g carbohydrate, 13.4 mg cholesterol, 44.8 mg sodium

STRAWBERRY GRAPE BREAD

A delicious, low-rising bread using fruit to replace sweetener and fat. The strawberries are pureed in a blender or food processor. Blueberries/raspberries, etc. may be substituted. I prefer using a white grape juice.

	Small	Medium	Large
strawberry puree	½ cup	¾ cup	1 cup
grape concentrate	⅓ cup	½ cup	⅔ cup
water	¼ cup	⅓ cup	½ cup
salt	¼ tsp.	⅓ tsp.	½ tsp.
vital gluten, optional	1 to 2 tbs.	1½ to 3 tbs.	2 to 4 tbs.
whole wheat flour	2 cups	3 cups	4 cups
yeast	1½ tsp.	2 tsp.	2½ tsp.

flour equivalents: *2 cups*   *3 cups*   *4 cups*
setting: light to medium   *timer: yes*

Nutritional analysis per 1 oz. slice   56.4 calories, 0.3 g fat (0.0 g sat fat), 2.8 g protein, 11.4 g carbohydrate, 0.0 mg cholesterol, 36.7 mg sodium

PINEAPPLE BANANA BREAD

Sinfully delicious yet still healthy and nutritious. Good toasted with yogurt/cream cheese and fresh fruit. Watch the dough for adequate moisture. Medium rise.

	Small	Medium	Large
mashed banana	⅓ cup	½ cup	⅔ cup
pineapple juice	¼ cup	½ cup	⅔ cup
crushed pineapple	⅓ cup	½ cup	⅔ cup
butter/margarine	1 tbs.	1½ tbs.	2 tbs.
salt	¼ tsp.	⅓ tsp.	½ tsp.
maple sugar/sucanet	1 tbs.	1½ tbs.	2 tbs.
vital gluten, optional	1 to 2 tbs.	1½ to 3 tbs.	2 to 4 tbs.
whole wheat flour	2 cups	3 cups	4 cups
yeast	1½ tsp.	2 tsp.	2½ tsp.

flour equivalents: *2 cups*   *3 cups*   *4 cups*
setting: light to medium   *timer: yes*

Nutritional analysis per 1 oz. slice   87.5 calories, 1.1 g fat (0.5 g sat fat), 2.9 g protein, 17.5 g carbohydrate, 2.1 mg cholesterol, 44.6 mg sodium

COCONUT BANANA BREAD

Four stars for this sweet breakfast or dessert bread.

	Small	Medium	Large
mashed bananas	¾ cup	1⅛ cups	1½ cups
milk/water	¼ cup	⅓ cup	½ cup
egg	1	1½	2
honey	1 tbs.	1½ tbs.	2 tbs.
coconut extract	1 tsp.	1½ tsp.	2 tsp.
salt	¼ tsp.	⅓ tsp.	½ tsp.
cinnamon	⅓ tsp.	½ tsp.	⅔ tsp.
nutmeg	¼ tsp.	⅓ tsp.	½ tsp.
shredded coconut	¼ cup	⅓ cup	½ cup
vital gluten, optional	1 to 2 tbs.	1½ to 3 tbs.	2 to 4 tbs.
whole wheat flour	2½ cups	3¾ cups	5 cups
yeast	1½ tsp.	2 tsp.	2½ tsp.
raisins	⅓ cup	½ cup	⅔ cup
flour equivalents:	*2½ cups*	*3¾ cups*	*5 cups*
setting: medium	*timer: no-raisin/mix cycle*		

Nutritional analysis per 1 oz. slice   112 calories, 1.3 g fat (0.6 g sat fat), 4.1 g protein, 22.5 g carbohydrate, 13.4 mg cholesterol, 47.1 mg sodium

HUNGARIAN ONION BREAD

Paprika adds flavor and color to this wonderful, low-rising, aromatic onion bread.

	Small	Medium	Large
water	⅔ cup	1 cup	1⅓ cups
fruit juice concentrate	1 tbs.	1½ tbs.	2 tbs.
finely diced onion	¼ cup	⅓ cup	½ cup
date/maple sugar	½ tsp.	⅔ tsp.	¾ tsp.
salt	⅛ tsp.	⅛+ tsp.	¼ tsp.
paprika	⅔ tsp.	¾ tsp.	1 tsp.
vital gluten, optional	1 to 2 tbs.	1½ to 3 tbs.	2 to 4 tbs.
whole wheat flour	2¼ cups	3⅓ cups	4½ cups
yeast	1 tsp.	1½ tsp.	2 tsp.

flour equivalents: *2¼ cups*   *3⅓ cups*   *4½ cups*
setting: medium   *timer: yes*

Nutritional analysis per 1 oz. slice   62.9 calories, 0.3 g fat (0.0 g sat fat), 3 g protein, 12.8 g carbohydrate, 0.0 mg cholesterol, 19.2 mg sodium

NUT BREADS

Several of the recipes in this section call for walnut or sunflower oil which add additional nutty flavoring to the bread. Fruit juice concentrates, applesauce or another vegetable oil may be substituted if you wish.

Please use any nut you desire as they all impart their own distinct tastes. Nuts which may be used include almonds, Brazil nuts, cashews, hazelnuts, macadamias, mixed, peanuts, pecans, pistachios or walnuts. While not really nuts, I also include sunflower kernels/seeds or pumpkin seeds in this category.

The amount of nuts included in the recipes may be increased if you wish. Some machines have difficulty cooking the bread completely with an abundance of nuts or dried fruits. My best advice is to experiment and find an amount which works well and suits your taste.

AMARANTH NUT BREAD

A densely textured loaf with a full, rich flavor which is good for sandwiches. Use walnuts, pecans or sunflower seeds.

	Small	**Medium**	**Large**
water	⅔ cup	1 cup	1⅓ cups
apple juice concentrate	2 tbs.	3 tbs.	¼ cup
honey	2 tbs.	3 tbs.	¼ cup
salt	¼ tsp.	⅓ tsp.	½ tsp.
vital gluten, optional	1 to 2 tbs.	1½ to 3 tbs.	2 to 4 tbs.
amaranth flour	⅓ cup	½ cup	⅔ cup
oat flakes	⅓ cup	½ cup	⅔ cup
whole wheat flour	1⅓ cups	2 cups	2⅔ cups
yeast	1½ tsp.	2 tsp.	2½ tsp.
chopped nuts	⅓ cup	½ cup	⅔ cup

flour equivalents: *2 cups*   *3 cups*   *4 cups*
setting: medium   *timer: no-raisin/mix cycle*

Nutritional analysis per 1 oz. slice   77.6 calories, 2.2 g fat (0.2 g sat fat), 3.3 g protein, 12 g carbohydrate, 0.0 mg cholesterol, 37 mg sodium

HONEY NUT OATMEAL BREAD

A wonderful whole grain version of an all-time favorite bread. Very low-rising, so I use the maximum amount of gluten.

	Small	**Medium**	**Large**
water/milk	¾ cup	1⅛ cups	1½ cups
fruit juice concentrate	1 tbs.	1½ tbs.	2 tbs.
honey	2 tbs.	3 tbs.	¼ cup
salt	¼ to ½ tsp.	⅓ to ¾ tsp.	½ to 1 tsp.
vital gluten, optional	1 to 2 tbs.	1½ to 3 tbs.	2 to 4 tbs.
rolled oats	½ cup	¾ cups	1 cup
whole wheat flour	1½ cups	2¼ cups	3 cups
yeast	1 tsp.	1½ tsp.	2 tsp.
chopped nuts	⅓ cup	½ cup	⅔ cup
flour equivalents:	*2 cups*	*3 cups*	*4 cups*
setting: medium	*timer: no-raisin/mix cycle*		

Nutritional analysis per 1 oz. slice   80.1 calories, 2.2 g fat (0.2 g sat fat), 3.4 g protein, 12.6 g carbohydrate, 0.0 mg cholesterol, 49 mg sodium

RAISIN WALNUT BREAD

A delicious bread. Any vegetable oil or fruit juice concentrate may be used if walnut oil is unavailable.

	Small	**Medium**	**Large**
buttermilk	½ cup	¾ cup	1 cup
walnut oil	2 tbs.	3 tbs.	¼ cup
honey/maple syrup	¼ cup	⅓ cup	½ cup
egg	1	1½	2
salt	½ tsp.	¾ tsp.	1 tsp.
baking soda	½ tsp.	¾ tsp.	1 tsp.
cinnamon	½ tsp.	¾ tsp.	1 tsp.
whole wheat flour	2 cups	3 cups	4 cups
yeast	1 tsp.	1½ tsp.	2 tsp.
raisins	⅓ cup	½ cup	⅔ cup
chopped walnuts	¼ cup	⅓ cup	½ cup
flour equivalents:	*2 cups*	*3 cups*	*4 cups*
setting: medium	*timer: no-raisin/mix cycle*		

Nutritional analysis per 1 oz. slice   116 calories, 3.6 g fat (0.7 g sat fat), 3.5 g protein, 19 g carbohydrate, 13.9 mg cholesterol, 119 mg sodium

PEANUT BUTTER AND JELLY BREAD

A high-rising loaf with the taste of peanut butter and jelly mixed right in. Use either smooth or chunky peanut butter. Due to peanut butter, the sides of the pan may need scraping. Watch moisture (see pages 13 and 14).

	Small	**Medium**	**Large**
water	¾ cup	1⅛ cups	1½ cups
peanut butter	⅓ cup	½ cup	⅔ cup
jelly	⅓ cup	½ cup	⅔ cup
maple/brown sugar	1 tbs.	1½ tbs.	2 tbs.
salt	⅓ tsp.	½ tsp.	⅔ tsp.
baking soda	½ tsp.	¾ tsp.	1 tsp.
vital gluten, optional	1 to 2 tbs.	1½ to 3 tbs.	2 to 4 tbs.
whole wheat flour	2¼ cups	3⅓ cups	4½ cups
yeast	1 tsp.	1½ tsp.	2 tsp.

flour equivalents: *2¼ cups*   *3⅓ cups*   *4½ cups*
setting: medium   *timer: yes*

Nutritional analysis per 1 oz. slice   92.5 calories, 1.9 g fat (0.3 g sat fat), 3.8 g protein, 16.3 g carbohydrate, 0.0 mg cholesterol, 89.5 mg sodium

PISTACHIO RAISIN BREAD

This is one of my favorite breads which has been adapted to whole grains. It's high-rising, tasty, and slices well.

	Small	**Medium**	**Large**
water	7⁄8 cup	1¼ cups	12⁄3 cups
honey	2 tbs.	3 tbs.	¼ cup
salt	⅓ tsp.	½ tsp.	⅔ tsp.
baking soda	½ tsp.	¾ tsp.	1 tsp.
vital gluten, optional	1 to 2 tbs.	1½ to 3 tbs.	2 to 4 tbs.
whole wheat flour	2¼ cups	3⅓ cups	4½ cups
yeast	1 tsp.	1½ tsp.	2 tsp.
———			
raisins	⅓ cup	½ cup	⅔ cup
pistachios	3 tbs.	¼ cup	⅓ cup

flour equivalents: 2¼ cups   3⅓ cups   4½ cups
setting: medium   timer: no-raisin/mix cycle

Nutritional analysis per 1 oz. slice   97.5 calories, 1.1 g fat (0.1 g sat fat), 3.3 g protein, 20.1 g carbohydrate, 0.0 mg cholesterol, 87 mg sodium

APPLE SUNFLOWER BREAD

good on sunflowe part "very subtle" apple flavor

A wonderful, nutty loaf of bread.

	Small	Medium	Large
apple juice	1 cup	1½ cups	2 cups
maple sugar/sucanet	1 tbs.	1½ tbs.	2 tbs.
salt	⅓ tsp.	½ tsp.	⅔ tsp.
baking soda/powder	½ tsp.	¾ tsp.	1 tsp.
sunflower seeds	½ cup	¾ cup	1 cup
vital gluten, optional	1 to 2 tbs.	1½ to 3 tbs.	2 to 4 tbs.
whole wheat flour	2¼ cups	3⅓ cups	4½ cups
yeast	1 tsp.	1½ tsp.	2 tsp.

flour equivalents:	2¾ cups	4 cups	5½ cups
setting: medium	timer: yes		

Nutritional analysis per 1 oz. slice   112 calories, 3.8 g fat (0.4 g sat fat), 4.3 g protein, 16.7 g carbohydrate, 0.0 mg cholesterol, 129 mg sodium

ALMOND RICE BREAD

Use your favorite rice in this bread, which should be lightly packed into the measuring cup. See pages 13 and 14 for tips on watching moisture, scraping pan.

	Small	**Medium**	**Large**
water	⅔ cup	1 cup	1⅓ cups
cooked rice	⅔ cup	1 cup	1⅓ cups
honey	2 tbs.	3 tbs.	¼ cup
salt	⅓ tsp.	½ tsp.	⅔ tsp.
garlic powder, optional	dash	⅛ tsp.	¼ tsp.
vital gluten, optional	1 to 2 tbs.	1½ to 3 tbs.	2 to 4 tbs.
whole wheat flour	2 cups	3 cups	4 cups
yeast	1½ tsp.	2 tsp	2½ tsp.
chopped almonds	3 tbs.	¼ cup	⅓ cup
flour equivalents:	*2⅔ cups*	*4 cups*	*5⅓ cups*
setting: medium	*timer: no-raisin/mix cycle*		

Nutritional analysis per 1 oz. slice 88.9 calories, 1.2 g fat (0.1 g sat fat), 3.2 g protein, 17.6 g carbohydrate, 0.0 mg cholesterol, 59 mg sodium

NUTTY RYE

A small amount of walnut oil adds extra flavor to this delicious rye.

	Small	**Medium**	**Large**
water/milk	1 cup	1½ cups	2 cups
walnut oil	2 tsp.	1 tbs.	1⅓ tbs.
honey/maple syrup	2 tbs.	3 tbs.	4 tbs.
salt	⅓ tsp.	½ tsp.	⅔ tsp.
baking soda	½ tsp.	¾ tsp.	1 tsp.
vital gluten, optional	1 to 2 tbs.	1½ to 3 tbs.	2 to 4 tbs.
rye flour	½ cup	¾ cup	1 cup
whole wheat flour	2 cups	3 cups	4 cups
yeast	1 tsp.	1½ tsp.	2 tsp.
——			
chopped nuts	⅓ cup	½ cup	¼ cup

flour equivalents:	*2½ cups*	*3¾ cups*	*5 cups*
setting: medium	*timer: no-raisin/mix cycle*		

Nutritional analysis per 1 oz. slice 106 calories, 2.8 g fat (0.3 g sat fat), 3.9 g protein, 18.1 g carbohydrate, 0.0 mg cholesterol, 75 mg sodium

RAISIN NUT BREAD

This is a densely textured loaf which rises about ¾ of the way up the pan.

	Small	**Medium**	**Large**
water/milk	¾ cup	1⅛ cups	1½ cups
egg	½	1	1
walnut oil	1 tbs.	1½ tbs.	2 tbs.
honey	2 tbs.	3 tbs.	4 tbs.
salt	⅓ tsp.	½ tsp.	⅔ tsp.
vital gluten, optional	1 to 2 tbs.	1½ to 3 tbs.	2 to 4 tbs.
whole wheat flour	2½ cups	3¾ cups	5 cups
yeast	1½ tsp.	2 tsp.	2½ tsp.
———			
raisins	⅓ cup	½ cup	⅔ cup
chopped walnuts	⅓ cup	½ cup	⅔ cup
flour equivalents:	*2½ cups*	*3¾ cups*	*5 cups*
setting: medium	*timer: no-raisin/mix cycle*		

Nutritional analysis per 1 oz. slice   125 calories, 3.2 g fat (0.4 g sat fat), 4.4 g protein, 21.4 g carbohydrate, 6.7 mg cholesterol, 51.7 mg sodium

APRICOT ALMOND BREAD

A delicate almond flavoring from the nuts makes this bread special.

almond extract ¼t

	Small	Medium	Large
buttermilk	⅞ cup	1¼ cups	1¾ cups
egg	1	1½	2
grated lemon peel	¼ tsp.	⅓ tsp.	½ tsp.
maple sugar/sucanet	2 tbs.	3 tbs.	¼ cup
salt	⅓ tsp.	½ tsp.	⅔ tsp.
baking soda	⅓ tsp.	½ tsp.	⅔ tsp.
vital gluten, optional	1 to 2 tbs.	1½ to 3 tbs.	2 to 4 tbs.
oat/wheat flakes	½ cup	¾ cup	1 cup
whole wheat flour	2 cups	3 cups	4 cups
yeast	1½ tsp.	2 tsp.	2½ tsp.
diced dried apricots	⅓ cup	½ cup	⅔ cup
chopped almonds	¼ cup	⅓ cup	½ cup
flour equivalents:	*2½ cups*	*3¾ cups*	*5 cups*
setting: medium	*timer: no-raisin/mix cycle*		

Nutritional analysis per 1 oz. slice   94.6 calories, 2 g fat (0.3 g sat fat), 4.4 g protein, 15.8 g carbohydrate, 13.8 mg cholesterol, 96.6 mg sodium

SUNFLOWER BREAD ~ok~

This nutty loaf rises nicely. Fruit juice concentrate may replace the oil if desired.

	Small	Medium	Large
milk/water	3/4 cup	1 1/8 cups	1 1/2 cups
egg	1	1 1/2	2
sunflower oil	1 tbs.	1 1/2 tbs.	2 tbs.
sucanet/maple sugar	1 tbs.	1 1/2 tbs.	2 tbs.
salt	1/3 tsp.	1/2 tsp.	2/3 tsp.
vital gluten, optional	1 to 2 tbs.	1 1/2 to 3 tbs.	2 to 4 tbs.
sunflower seeds	1/2 cup	3/4 cup	1 cup
whole wheat flour	2 cups	3 cups	4 cups
yeast	1 1/2 tsp.	2 tsp.	2 1/2 tsp.

flour equivalents: *2 1/2 cups*   *3 3/4 cups*   *5 cups*
setting: medium   *timer: no (milk, egg)*

Nutritional analysis per 1 oz. slice   112 calories, 5 g fat (0.6 g sat fat), 4.9 g protein, 13.4 g carbohydrate, 13.5 mg cholesterol, 113 mg sodium

WALNUT ONION BREAD

A low- to medium-rising loaf of bread with superior taste.

	Small	Medium	Large
water	¾ cup	1⅛ cups	1½ cups
diced onion	¼ cup	⅓ cup	½ cup
walnut oil	1 tbs.	1½ tbs.	2 tbs.
honey	1 tbs.	1½ tbs.	2 tbs.
salt	⅓ tsp.	½ tsp.	⅔ tsp.
rosemary or basil	¼ tsp.	⅓ tsp.	½ tsp.
vital gluten, optional	1 to 2 tbs.	1½ to 3 tbs.	2 to 4 tbs.
rye flour	½ cup	¾ cup	1 cup
whole wheat flour	2 cups	3 cup	4 cups
yeast	1½ tsp.	2 tsp.	2½ tsp.
chopped walnuts	¼ cup	⅓ cup	½ cup
flour equivalents:	*2½ cups*	*3¾ cups*	*5 cups*
setting: medium	*timer: no-raisin/mix cycle*		

Nutritional analysis per 1 oz. slice 94.1 calories, 2.3 g fat (0.3 g sat fat), 3.6 g protein, 16 g carbohydrate, 0.0 mg cholesterol, 49.4 mg sodium

BANANA COCONUT NUT BREAD

A nicely rising loaf even without the vital gluten. Watch the moisture on this one.

	Small	**Medium**	**Large**
mashed banana	½ cup	¾ cup	1 cup
buttermilk	½ cup	¾ cup	1 cup
egg	1	1½	2
maple sugar/sucanet	2 tbs.	3 tbs.	¼ cup
salt	⅓ tsp.	½ tsp.	⅔ tsp.
baking soda	⅓ tsp.	½ tsp.	⅔ tsp.
coconut	¼ cup	⅓ cup	½ cup
vital gluten, optional	1 to 2 tbs.	1½ to 3 tbs.	2 to 4 tbs.
whole wheat flour	2½ cups	3⅔ cups	5 cups
yeast	1½ tsp.	2 tsp.	2½ tsp.
―――			
chopped nuts	⅓ cup	½ cup	⅔ cup

flour equivalents: *2½ cups*   *3¾ cups*   *5 cups*
setting: medium   *timer: no-raisin/mix cycle*

Nutritional analysis per 1 oz. slice   113 calories, 2.7 g fat (0.3 g sat fat), 4.8 g protein, 19 g carbohydrate, 13.6 mg cholesterol, 78 mg sodium

CHOCOLATE NUT BREAD

A delicious chocolate raisin bread.

	Small	**Medium**	**Large**
buttermilk	¾ cup	1⅛ cups	1½ cups
egg	1	1½	2
unsweetened cocoa	1 tbs.	1½ tbs.	2 tbs.
maple sugar/sucanet	2 tbs.	3 tbs.	¼ cup
salt	⅓ tsp.	½ tsp.	⅔ tsp.
baking soda	⅓ tsp.	½ tsp.	⅔ tsp.
vital gluten, optional	1 to 2 tbs.	1½ to 3 tbs.	2 to 4 tbs.
wheat/oat flakes	½ cup	¾ cup	1 cup
whole wheat flour	2 cups	3 cups	4 cups
yeast	1½ tsp.	2 tsp.	2½ tsp.
raisins	⅓ cup	½ cup	⅔ cup
chopped nuts	⅓ cup	½ cup	⅔ cup
flour equivalents:	*2½ cups*	*3¾ cups*	*5 cups*
setting: medium	*timer: no-raisin/mix cycle*		

Nutritional analysis per 1 oz. slice   129 calories, 2.7 g fat (0.4 g sat fat), 5.5 g protein, 22.1 g carbohydrate, 13.9 mg cholesterol, 85.4 mg sodium

POULSBO BREAD

A favorite bread which has been adapted to whole grains. The original Poulsbo bread was developed by a bakery in Poulsbo, Washington based on Biblical references to bread. The real keys are the multi-grain cereal (7, 9 or 12) and the sunflower seeds.

	Small	Medium	Large
water/milk	¾ cup	1⅛ cups	1½ cups
fruit juice concentrate	1 tbs.	1½ tbs.	2 tbs.
molasses/honey	1⅓ tbs.	2 tbs.	2⅔ tbs.
salt	½ tsp.	¾ tsp.	1 tsp.
vital gluten, optional	1 to 2 tbs.	1½ to 3 tbs.	2 to 4 tbs.
7 grain cereal	½ cup	¾ cup	1 cup
whole wheat flour	2 cups	3 cups	4 cups
powdered buttermilk	1 tbs.	1½ tbs.	2 tbs.
yeast	1 tsp.	1½ tsp.	2 tsp.
sunflower seeds	⅓ cup	½ cup	⅔ cup
flour equivalents:	*2½ cups*	*3¾ cups*	*5 cups*
setting: medium	*timer: no-raisin/mix cycle*		

Nutritional analysis per 1 oz. slice   87.9 calories, 0.9 g fat (0.1 g sat fat), 3.9 g protein, 16.4 g carbohydrate, 0.0 mg cholesterol, 80.8 mg sodium

CINNAMON RAISIN NUT BREAD

A delicious bread whether toasted for breakfast or used in a sandwich.

	Small	**Medium**	**Large**
milk/water	⅞ cup	1¼ cups	1¾ cups
egg	1	1½	2
maple sugar/sucanet	2 tbs.	3 tbs.	¼ cup
cinnamon	½ tsp.	¾ tsp.	1 tsp.
salt	⅓ tsp.	½ tsp.	⅔ tsp.
vital gluten, optional	1 to 2 tbs.	1½ to 3 tbs.	2 to 4 tbs.
wheat/oat flakes	½ cup	¾ cup	1 cup
whole wheat flour	2 cups	3 cups	4 cups
yeast	1½ tsp.	2 tsp.	2½ tsp.
———			
raisins	¼ cup	⅓ cup	½ cup
chopped nuts	⅓ cup	½ cup	⅔ cup

flour equivalents: 2½ cups   3¾ cups   5 cups
setting: medium   timer: *no-raisin/mix cycle*

Nutritional analysis per 1 oz. slice   124 calories, 2.6 g fat (0.3 g sat fat), 5.5 g protein, 20.9 g carbohydrate, 13.5 mg cholesterol, 60.5 mg sodium

HAWAIIAN MACADAMIA NUT BREAD

This is wonderful — sweet but can still be used for sandwiches if desired.

	Small	Medium	Large
buttermilk	1 cup	1½ cups	2 cups
egg	1	1½	2
fruit juice concentrate	1 tbs.	1½ tbs.	2 tbs.
maple sugar/sucanet	2 tbs.	3 tbs.	¼ cup
salt	½ tsp.	¾ tsp.	1 tsp.
baking soda	⅓ tsp.	½ tsp.	⅔ tsp.
vital gluten, optional	1 to 2 tbs.	1½ to 3 tbs.	2 to 4 tbs.
whole wheat flour	2½ cups	3¾ cups	5 cups
yeast	1½ tsp.	2 tsp.	2½ tsp.
———			
chopped macadamias	⅓ cup	½ cup	⅔ cup

flour equivalents: *2½ cups*   *3¾ cups*   *5 cups*
setting: medium   *timer: no-raisin/mix cycle*

Nutritional analysis per 1 oz. slice   108 calories, 3.5 g fat (0.6 g sat fat), 4.4 g protein, 16.1 g carbohydrate, 13.9 mg cholesterol, 110 mg sodium

DATE NUT BREAD

A chocolate-flavored date bread. This makes a medium- to high-rising loaf.

	Small	**Medium**	**Large**
water/milk	¾ cup	1⅛ cups	1½ cups
egg	1	1½	2
unsweetened cocoa	1 tbs.	1½ tbs.	2 tbs.
maple sugar/sucanet	2 tbs.	3 tbs.	¼ cup
salt	⅓ tsp.	½ tsp.	⅔ tsp.
vital gluten, optional	1 to 2 tbs.	1½ to 3 tbs.	2 to 4 tbs.
whole wheat flour	2½ cups	3¾ cups	5 cups
yeast	1½ tsp.	2 tsp.	2½ tsp.
chopped dates	⅓ cup	½ cup	⅔ cup
chopped nuts	⅓ cup	½ cup	⅔ cup
flour equivalents:	*2½ cups*	*3¾ cups*	*5 cups*
setting: medium	*timer: no-raisin/mix cycle*		

Nutritional analysis per 1 oz. slice   107 calories, 2.5 g fat (0.3 g sat fat), 4.5 g protein, 18.2 g carbohydrate, 13.4 mg cholesterol, 55.6 mg sodium

APPLE DATE NUT BREAD

An excellent very aromatic bread with lots of rich flavor.

	Small	Medium	Large
apple juice	7/8 cup	1¼ cups	1½ cups
honey	1 tbs.	1½ tbs.	2 tbs.
salt	¼ tsp.	⅓ tsp.	½ tsp.
cinnamon	¼ tsp.	⅓ tsp.	½ tsp.
vital gluten, optional	1 to 2 tbs.	1½ to 3 tbs.	2 to 4 tbs.
whole wheat flour	2½ cups	3¾ cups	5 cups
yeast	1 tsp.	1½ tsp.	2 tsp.
diced, peeled apple	¼ cup	⅓ cup	½ cup
chopped dates	2 to 3 tbs.	¼ cup	⅓ cup
chopped nuts	¼ cup	⅓ cup	½ cup

flour equivalents: *2½ cups*   *3¾ cups*   *5 cups*
setting: medium   *timer: no-raisin/mix cycle*

Nutritional analysis per 1 oz. slice   94.4 calories, 1.5 g fat (0.1 g sat fat), 3.8 g protein, 17.9 g carbohydrate, 0.0 mg cholesterol, 37.2 mg sodium

MEXICAN DATE PECAN BREAD

A wonderful, sweet bread which makes great toast or French toast. Rises well.

	Small	Medium	Large
milk	3/4 cup	1 1/8 cups	1 1/2 cups
egg	1	1 1/2	2
fruit juice concentrate	1 tbs.	1 1/2 tbs.	2 tbs.
salt	1/4 tsp.	1/3 tsp.	1/2 tsp.
maple sugar/sucanet	2 tbs.	2 1/2 tbs.	3 tbs.
cinnamon	1/2 tsp.	2/3 tsp.	3/4 tsp.
nutmeg	1/8 tsp.	1/8+ tsp.	1/4 tsp.
vital gluten, optional	1 to 2 tbs.	1 1/2 to 3 tbs.	2 to 4 tbs.
whole wheat flour	2 1/4 cups	3 1/3 cups	4 1/2 cups
yeast	1 1/2 tsp.	2 tsp.	2 1/2 tsp.
———			
chopped dates	1/3 cup	1/2 cup	2/3 cup
chopped pecans	1/4 cup	1/3 cup	1/2 cup
flour equivalents:	*2 1/4 cups*	*3 1/3 cups*	*4 1/2 cups*
setting: medium	*timer: no-raisin/mix cycle*		

Nutritional analysis per 1 oz. slice 96.3 calories, 1.8 g fat (0.2 g sat fat), 4 g protein, 17.2 g carbohydrate, 13.5 mg cholesterol, 46.6 mg sodium

MACADAMIA NUT BREAD

This is a "must try" — a delicious sweet bread which is great toasted for breakfast or brunch or served with dessert. Medium to high rise.

	Small	Medium	Large
buttermilk	¾ cup	1⅛ cups	1½ cups
egg	1	1½	2
honey/maple syrup	2 tbs.	3 tbs.	¼ cup
salt	⅓ tsp.	½ tsp.	⅔ tsp.
baking soda	¼ tsp.	⅓ tsp.	½ tsp.
ground ginger	¼ tsp.	⅓ tsp.	½ tsp.
oats/wheat flakes	½ cup	¾ cup	1 cup
vital gluten, optional	1 to 2 tbs.	1½ to 3 tbs.	2 to 4 tbs.
coconut flakes	¼ cup	⅓ cup	½ cup
whole wheat flour	2 cups	3 cups	4 cups
yeast	1½ tsp.	2 tsp.	2½ tsp.
chopped macadamias	⅓ cup	½ cup	⅔ cup
flour equivalents:	*2½ cups*	*3⅓ cups*	*4½ cups*
setting: medium	*timer: no-raisin/mix cycle*		

Nutritional analysis per 1 oz. slice   114 calories, 4 g fat (1.1 g sat fat), 4.2 g protein, 16.7 g carbohydrate, 13.7 mg cholesterol, 81.7 mg sodium

SQUAW BREAD

An often-requested sweet bread adapted to whole grains. Medium to high rise.

	Small	**Medium**	**Large**
water	¾ cup	1⅛ cups	1½ cups
egg	1	1½	2
fruit juice concentrate	1 tbs.	1½ tbs.	2 tbs.
honey	1 tbs.	1½ tbs.	2 tbs.
brown/maple sugar	1 tbs.	1½ tbs.	2 tbs.
raisins	1 tbs.	1½ tbs.	2 tbs.
salt	½ tsp.	⅔ tsp.	1 tsp.
vital gluten, optional	1 to 2 tbs.	1½ to 3 tbs.	2 to 4 tbs.
rye flour	½ cup	¾ cup	1 cup
whole wheat flour	2 cups	3 cups	4 cups
yeast	1½ tsp.	2 tsp.	2½ tsp.
sunflower seeds	¼ cup	⅓ cup	½ cup
flour equivalents:	*2½ cups*	*3¾ cups*	*5 cups*
setting: medium	*timer: no-raisin/mix cycle*		

Nutritional analysis per 1 oz. slice   99.6 calories, 2.4 g fat (0.3 g sat fat), 4.2 g protein, 16.6 g carbohydrate, 13.3 mg cholesterol, 104 mg sodium

SUNFLOWER OATMEAL BREAD

A DRH likes

Wow! What a combination.

	Small	**Medium**	**Large**
water/milk	⅔ cup	1 cup	1⅓ cups
fruit juice concentrate	1 tbs.	1½ tbs.	2 tbs.
honey	2 tbs.	3 tbs.	¼ cup
salt	¼ tsp.	⅓ tsp.	½ tsp.
baking soda	½ tsp.	¾ tsp.	1 tsp.
sunflower seeds	⅓ cup	½ cup	⅔ cup
oats	½ cup	¾ cup	1 cup
vital gluten, optional	1 to 2 tbs.	1½ to 3 tbs.	2 to 4 tbs.
whole wheat flour	1½ cups	2¼ cups	3 cups
yeast	1 tsp.	1½ tsp.	2 tsp.

flour equivalents: 2⅓ cups 3½ cups 4⅔ cups
setting: medium   *timer: yes with water*

Nutritional analysis per 1oz. slice 64.1 calories, 0.7 g fat (0.1 g sat. fat), 2.8 g protein, 12.4 g carbohydrate, 0.0 mg cholesterol, 67.7 mg sodium

ALMOND POPPY SEED BREAD

An outstanding bread for dessert or brunch. I prefer the honey over the maple syrup. Rises well. Watch the moisture.

	Small	**Medium**	**Large**
buttermilk	7/8 cup	1¼ cups	1¾ cups
almond extract	1 tbs.	1½ tbs.	2 tbs.
honey/maple syrup	2 tbs.	3 tbs.	4 tbs.
salt	¼ tsp.	⅓ tsp.	½ tsp.
poppy seeds	1 tbs.	1½ tbs.	2 tbs.
baking soda	¼ tsp.	⅓ tsp.	½ tsp.
vital gluten, optional	1 to 2 tbs.	1½ to 3 tbs.	2 to 4 tbs.
whole wheat flour	2¼ cups	3⅓ cups	4½ cups
yeast	1 tsp.	1½ tsp.	2 tsp.
—			
chopped almonds	⅓ cup	½ cup	⅔ cup
flour equivalents:	*2¼ cups*	*3⅓ cups*	*4½ cups*
setting: medium	*timer: no-raisin/mix cycle*		

Nutritonal analysis per 1 oz. slice 99.2 calories, 2.6 g fat (0.3 g sat fat), 4.1 g protein, 16.1 g carbohydrate, 0.5 mg cholesterol, 85.8 mg sodium

BLACK WALNUT BREAD

Black walnuts have very distinctive, rich flavor which is quite different than English walnuts. This bread takes full advantage of the distinctive black walnut taste.

	Small	Medium	Large
buttermilk	¾ cup	1 cup less 1 tbs.	1⅛ cups
black walnut extract	1 tbs.	1½ tbs.	2 tbs.
honey	2 tbs.	2½ tbs.	3 tbs.
egg	1	1½	2
salt	¼ tsp.	⅓ tsp.	½ tsp.
baking soda	¼ tsp.	⅓ tsp.	½ tsp.
coconut flakes	¼ cup	⅓ cup	½ cup
vital gluten, optional	1 to 2 tbs.	1½ to 3 tbs.	2 to 4 tbs.
oats	½ cup	¾ cup	1 cup
whole wheat flour	2 cups	3 cups	4 cups
yeast	1½ tsp.	2 tsp.	2½ tsp.
chopped black walnuts	⅓ cup	½ cup	⅔ cup
flour equivalents:	*2½ cups*	*3¾ cups*	*5 cups*

setting: medium   timer: no (buttermilk, egg)

Nutritional analysis per 1 oz. slice   111 calories, 3.2 g fat (0.8 g sat fat), 4.8 g protein, 16.6 g carbohydrate, 13.7 mg cholesterol, 69.5 mg sodium

CRACKED WHEAT ALMOND BREAD

The cracked wheat must sit in the liquid for at least one hour (see page 21). A great, low-rising bread.

	Small	**Medium**	**Large**
water	1 cup	1½ cups	2 cups
cracked wheat	½ cup	¾ cup	1 cup
fruit juice concentrate	1 tbs.	1½ tbs.	2 tbs.
almond extract	1 tbs.	1½ tbs.	2 tbs.
salt	⅓ tsp.	½ tsp.	⅔ tsp.
baking soda	½ tsp.	¾ tsp.	1 tsp.
vital gluten, optional	1 to 2 tbs.	1½ to 3 tbs.	2 to 4 tbs.
wheat flour	2 cups	3 cups	4 cups
yeast	1 tsp.	1½ tsp.	2 tsp.
chopped almonds	⅓ cup	½ cup	⅔ cup
flour equivalents:	*2½ cups*	*3¾ cups*	*5 cups*
setting: medium	*timer: yes*		

Nutritional analysis per 1 oz. slice   68 calories, 0.4 g fat (0.0 g sat fat), 3.2 g protein, 13.8 g carbohydrate, 0.0 mg cholesterol, 76.1 mg sodium

ORANGE NUT BREAD

This is one of our favorite combinations. Use your favorite nuts.

	Small	Medium	Large
buttermilk	¾ cup	1⅛ cups	1½ cups
orange juice concentrate	2 tbs.	3 tbs.	4 tbs.
honey	2 tbs.	3 tbs.	4 tbs.
egg	1	1½	2
salt	⅓ tsp.	½ tsp.	⅔ tsp.
baking soda	¼ to ½ tsp.	⅓ to ¾ tsp.	½ to 1 tsp.
oats	½ cup	¾ cup	1 cup
vital gluten, optional	1 to 2 tbs.	1½ to 3 tbs.	2 to 4 tbs.
whole wheat flour	2¼ cups	3⅓ cups	4½ cups
yeast	1½ tsp.	2 tsp.	2½ tsp.
chopped nuts	⅓ cup	½ cup	⅔ cup
dried cranberries, optional	¼ cup	⅓ cup	½ cup
flour equivalents:	*2¾ cups*	*4+ cups*	*5½ cups*
setting: medium	*timer: no-raisin/mix cycle*		

Nutritional analysis per 1 oz. slice 93.5 calories, 0.9 g fat (0.2 g sat fat), 4.3 g protein, 18.1 g carbohydrate, 13.7 mg cholesterol, 77.8 mg sodium

CINNAMON CHOCOLATE BREAD

The combination of cinnamon and chocolate is common in Mexican cooking.

	Small	**Medium**	**Large**
milk/water	¾ cup	1⅛ cups	1½ cups
honey	2 tbs.	3 tbs.	¼ cup
eggs	1	1½	2
salt	⅓ tsp.	½ tsp.	⅔ tsp.
unsweetened cocoa	1 tbs.	1½ tbs.	2 tbs.
cinnamon	¼ tsp.	⅓ tsp.	½ tsp.
vital gluten, optional	1 to 2 tbs.	1½ to 3 tbs.	2 to 4 tbs.
whole wheat flour	2¼ cups	3⅓ cups	4½ cups
yeast	1½ tsp.	2 tsp.	2½ tsp.
chopped nuts	⅓ cup	½ cup	⅔ cup

flour equivalents: 2¼ cups   3⅓ cups   4½ cups
setting: medium   *timer: no-raisin/mix cycle*

Nutritional analysis per 1 oz. slice   90.7 calories, 1.8 g fat (0.3 g sat fat), 4.3 g protein, 15.6 g carbohydrate, 13.6 mg cholesterol, 61.1 mg sodium

MAPLE WALNUT BREAD

Wow! It is worth buying walnut oil to enjoy in this nutty tasting bread. A medium-to high-rising loaf, this slices nicely.

1 egg

	Small	Medium	Large
water	3/4 cup	1 1/8 cups	1 1/2 cups
walnut oil	1 tbs.	1 1/2 tbs.	2 tbs.
maple syrup	2 tbs.	3 tbs.	1/4 cup
cinnamon	1/4 tsp.	1/3 tsp.	1/2 tsp.
salt	1/4 tsp.	1/3 tsp.	1/2 tsp.
vital gluten, optional	1 to 2 tbs.	1 1/2 to 3 tbs.	2 to 4 tbs.
whole wheat flour	2 1/4 cups	3 1/3 cups	4 1/2 cups
yeast	1 tsp.	1 1/2 tsp.	2 tsp.
——			
chopped walnuts	1/3 cup	1/2 cup	2/3 cup

flour equivalent: 2 1/4 cups 3 1/3 cups 4 1/2 cups
setting: medium *timer: no-raisin/mix cycle*

Nutritional analysis per 1 oz. slice 95 calories, 3 g fat (0.4 g sat fat), 3.8 g protein, 14.4 g carbohydrate, 0.0 mg cholesterol, 38.6 mg sodium

SOURCES

Call for a free catalog or ordering information:

Arrowhead Mills, Inc. (806) 346-0730 (grains and flours)
Cal-Gar Corp. (201) 691-2928 (Gold Rush Sourdough Starter)
Garden Spot Distributors (800) 829-5100 (grains, flours, cereals)
Gibson's Healthful Living (800) 388-6844 (grains, bread machines, mills)
Great Valley Mills (800) 688-6455 (stone ground flours, etc.)
Jaffee Bros. Inc. (619) 749-1282 (grains, flours, and other food items)
K-Tec (800) 288-6455 (grain mills, grains, cereals, other bread baking items)
King Arthur Flour (802) 649-3881 (flours, grains, starters, other items)
Mountain Woods (800) 835-0479 (Fiddle Bow Bread Knives)
Walnut Acres (800) 433-3998 (organic farm: flours, grains, etc.)

no longer published

For information about *The Bread Machine Newsletter* by Donna R. German:
976 Houston Northcutt Blvd., Suite 3
Mt. Pleasant, SC 29464

Write for a complimentary review copy or with any questions you may have related to bread machine baking.

INDEX

SERVE CREATIVE, EASY, NUTRITIOUS MEALS WITH NITTY GRITTY® COOKBOOKS

Extra-Special Crockery Pot Recipes
Clay Cookery
Marinades
Deep-Fried Indulgences
Cooking with Parchment Paper
The Garlic Cookbook
Flatbreads From Around the World
From Your Ice Cream Maker
Favorite Cookie Recipes
Cappuccino/Espresso: The Book of Beverages
Indoor Grilling
Slow Cooking
The Best Pizza is Made at Home
The Well Dressed Potato
Convection Oven Cookery
The Steamer Cookbook
The Pasta Machine Cookbook
The Versatile Rice Cooker

The Dehydrator Cookbook
The Bread Machine Cookbook
The Bread Machine Cookbook II
The Bread Machine Cookbook III
The Bread Machine Cookbook IV
The Bread Machine Cookbook V
Worldwide Sourdoughs From Your Bread Machine
Recipes for the Pressure Cooker
The New Blender Book
The Sandwich Maker Cookbook
Waffles
The Coffee Book
The Juicer Book
The Juicer Book II
Bread Baking (traditional), revised
No Salt, No Sugar, No Fat Cookbook

Cooking for 1 or 2
Quick and Easy Pasta Recipes
The 9x13 Pan Cookbook
Chocolate Cherry Tortes and Other Lowfat Delights
Low Fat American Favorites
Now That's Italian!
Fabulous Fiber Cookery
Low Salt, Low Sugar, Low Fat Desserts
Healthy Cooking on the Run
Healthy Snacks for Kids
Muffins, Nut Breads and More
The Wok
New Ways to Enjoy Chicken
Favorite Seafood Recipes
New International Fondue Cookbook

Write or call for our free catalog.
BRISTOL PUBLISHING ENTERPRISES, INC.
P.O. Box 1737, San Leandro, CA 94577
(800) 346-4889; in California (510) 895-4461